INTRODUCTION

Megawords introduces procedures for teaching the reading and spelling of multisyllabic words through a multisensory approach. The program is the result of our experience teaching learning disabled children and adults. However, the techniques described will be useful to teachers of any population for which the goal is word attack skills for words with more than one syllable.

In working with learning disabled students, adults, and others with reading and spelling difficulties, we noted a lack of appropriate materials for teaching the reading and spelling of multisyllabic words. Numerous programs exist for instruction of phonic generalizations found in one-syllable words. While many materials include phonic elements of multisyllabic word patterns, few provide a format to assess skills, pinpoint weaknesses, teach required subskills, and monitor progress systematically. The dearth of materials for teaching skills in this area is a major problem for teachers whose students have reached a fourth- or fifth-grade reading and/or spelling level. Many students have difficulty advancing beyond this level, at which mastery of multisyllabic words becomes necessary. Our need to create a program to teach the more advanced reading and spelling skills became paramount.

At first it seemed impossible to design a structured format for teaching multisyllabic words because of their phonic complexity. As we developed the program, however, it became clear that the English language could be analyzed into components that demonstrate an amazing degree of regularity and consistency. We developed controlled word lists that build sequentially on phonic and structural elements. Some words are appropriately placed on more than one list. Some lists include words with phonic elements that are not focused on until later in the sequence. Though the lists are not perfectly inclusive or exclusive, each emphasizes a significant and recurring phonic element of the English language. Students can be encouraged to add new words to lists as they study them.

GENERAL DESCRIPTION OF *MEGAWORDS*

Megawords combines several principles found to be effective in teaching students with language learning difficulties. These principles, combined and specifically applied to the teaching of multisyllabic words, make *Megawords* unique.

- *Megawords* teaches phonic regularities. The lists are structured according to phonic elements. This approach stresses the teaching of rules and generalizations as a tool for sounding out and spelling unfamiliar words. The words are not to be taught as sight words unless indicated.

- *Megawords* is multisensory. Specific teaching instructions are provided to ensure that students use their auditory, visual, and kinesthetic modalities when learning a skill. The process of seeing, saying, hearing, and writing is a major key to success. Thus, the students practice spelling the words as they learn to read them.

- *Megawords* is systematic. There is no guesswork as to what students need to be taught or when to advance them through the program. A skills Check Test assesses each student's skills by pinpointing deficits and identifying specific instructional goals. Systematic monitoring of progress by use of the Accuracy Checklist for recording accuracy and of the Proficiency Graph for recording reading rate is an integral part of the program.

- *Megawords* is task analytic. The words on each list are analyzed and broken down into their component subskills and presented in sequential learning steps. Though the final objective is for students to read and spell the words with automaticity, they often need specific instruction on the intervening steps. When they use this method, their success is guaranteed.

- *Megawords* is adaptable to the individual's needs. The task analytic nature of the program makes this possible. Some students may master a word list with minimal drill on the sequential learning steps. Others will require more instructional time on each step. Goals for accuracy and proficiency are determined on an individual basis.

- *Megawords* is adaptable to the teacher's needs. It may be used for classroom instruction or for one-to-one tutoring. In a classroom setting, students can chart and graph their own progress. They can also learn to time each other for proficiency and to test each other for accuracy. The charts and graphs allow easy monitoring of the progress recorded by the students. The word lists can serve as a supplement to the regular reading program and the sequence can be adapted to correspond to other materials.

- *Megawords* encourages student involvement. Most students are motivated to progress when goals are identified for them. The structured format of this program specifies what is to be learned and how well it is to be learned. Because students can monitor their own progress, they can move at their own pace rather than that of the class average. Group or individual rewards for mastering skills can be used to motivate students.

- *Megawords* may be used by paraprofessionals. Teacher's aides, volunteers, and peer tutors can easily follow the instructions. Explanations for administration of the Check Test, teaching concepts, and monitoring progress are written in clear and simple language. With a modicum of effort, teachers can supervise and train paraprofessionals to use *Megawords* so that instruction can be individualized.

OVERVIEW OF TEACHING STRATEGIES

Megawords teaches the reading, spelling, and contextual use of multisyllabic words through a systematic progression of skills. Each book focuses on a distinct group of phonic skills; teaching strategies throughout the program are uniform.

For multisensory teaching to be successful, students need to practice spelling words while they learn to read them. This procedure provides the necessary simultaneous input through all the processing channels (visual, auditory, and kinesthetic). However, the approach used to teach spelling to low-skilled students differs in emphasis from that used to teach them reading. For reading, the goal is to teach students word attack skills that they can apply to decoding (sounding out) unfamiliar words. Thus, it is desirable to present to the students a large number of words that they may never have seen before in order to challenge their understanding of the concepts taught.

In contrast, the number of words required for spelling mastery should be limited for low-skilled students because spelling is a much more complex skill. Multisyllabic words frequently contain the schwa sound, which can be spelled with any of the five vowels. While this does not typically present a reading problem for students, it is a major barrier for those students who must learn to spell phonetically. This difficulty also applies to other vowel and consonant sounds that can be spelled in more than one way. The spelling task is usually further complicated by students' not receiving immediate feedback on their performances. For these reasons it is not feasible for severely learning disabled or low-skilled students to learn the correct spelling of all the words on the lists. Rather, students should learn to spell a limited number of useful words *well*. On each list we identify with an asterisk *practical spelling words* that the students are likely to use in writing. Teachers and students should feel free to add to or delete these words to suit their needs.

The procedures for using the *Megawords* materials are outlined below. You should familiarize yourself with these teaching strategies before using the program.

ASSESSMENT OF READING AND SPELLING SKILLS

Each book contains a detailed Check Test, which will specifically pinpoint skill deficits and, thus, identify which lists should be the focal point of instruction. This Check Test should be given as a pretest before students start a book. It can be readministered after students complete the book if posttest scores are desired. The Book 6 Check Test and instructions for administration are found on pages 10-11.

LEARNING STEPS

A discussion of relevant rules and concepts introduces each list. Six sequential learning steps follow; they lead to the final objective — reading and spelling words with automaticity. This task breakdown analyzes words according to their phonetic elements and then presents them in a parts-to-whole fashion.

Worksheets for each learning step enable students to acquire the necessary skills gradually. In this way, they experience greater success. Some students may proceed through all the steps rapidly or may even bypass some steps. Others may require prolonged drill and supplemental activities. Pacing will depend on the individual student's needs.

The Task Breakdown for Teaching the Coding of Multisyllabic Words on page 4 summarizes the six learning steps that are the backbone of *Megawords*. Each step includes both a decoding (reading) and an encoding (spelling) task. The left half of the chart indicates the decoding subskills; the right half, the encoding subskills. The tasks required at each step are as follows:

STEP 1. Work with the Isolated Word Parts

Drill on the isolated word parts is a necessary first step. This may entail identifying types of syllables or working on prefixes, suffixes, or special vowel and consonant combinations. Worksheets require the students both to read and spell the word parts. In addition, we recommend that students get additional practice on the isolated parts by using drill cards. Instructions for using drill cards in teaching specific skills are provided in each book.

STEP 2. Work with the Combined Word Parts

For this step, students are required to recognize word parts within words, combine them, and read a whole word. The reverse procedure is required for spelling: the teacher dictates a whole word and the student must isolate and spell the word parts. At first, students should say the isolated word parts aloud before spelling them. Eventually, they can say them to themselves. Practice with common spelling patterns for the schwa sound is included when relevant. This step is crucial and should not be bypassed.

Students are sometimes asked to mark vowels in words with an unaccented syllable. Some dictionaries list both the schwa and the soft-*i* sounds as acceptable pronunciations and some vary on the choice. Regional accents also affect the pronunciation of these words. For these reasons, do not insist that students always know the technically correct vowel sound as long as they can decode the word.

In Step 2 — Reading, words are presented as detached syllables as an intermediate step to help students identify the correct vowel sound before having to tackle whole words. You may notice that syllabication in *Megawords* is closer to that used for hyphenation than that found in pronunciation guides in a dictionary (*chat-ter* rather than /chat•er/, *dis-cus-sion* rather than /dis•kəsh•ən/). Syllabication is presented as simply as possible to avoid confusing the student with technical syllabication rules.

STEP 3. Work with the Whole Word

If students have had sufficient drill on Steps 1 and 2, reading and spelling the whole word should be relatively easy. For reading, they practice applying relevant word attack skills. Worksheets require them to divide whole words into syllables and to pronounce them. The spelling worksheets for Step 3 focus on words frequently used in writing. Students practice spelling the recurring phonic elements in common words. Spelling rules and generalizations are also presented in Step 3. Proofreading, the detection and correction of spelling errors, is a necessary and important skill for all students. Step 3 exercises provide practice in this skill.

TASK BREAKDOWN FOR TEACHING THE CODING OF MULTISYLLABIC WORDS

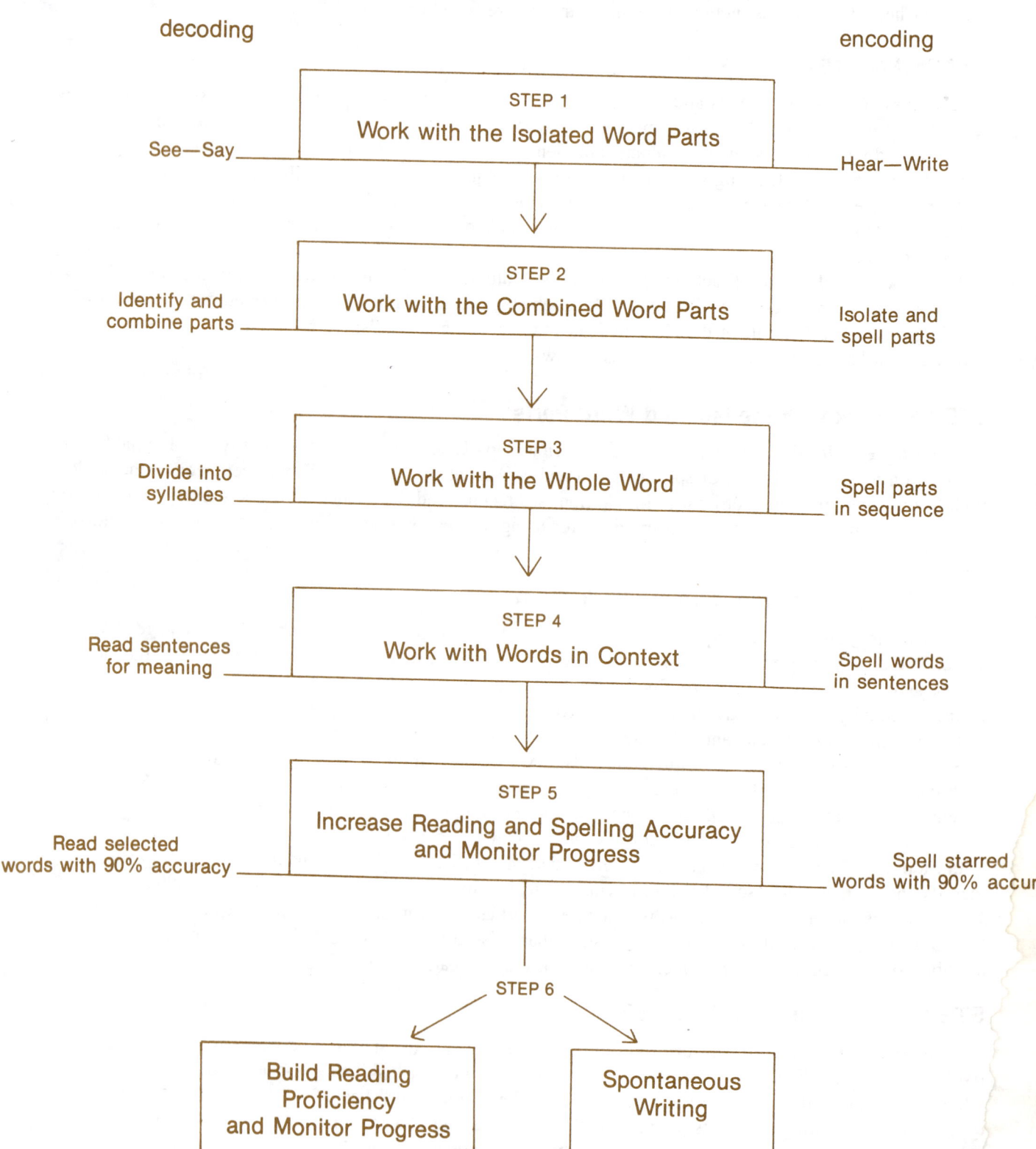

decoding

encoding

STEP 1
Work with the Isolated Word Parts

See—Say

Hear—Write

STEP 2
Work with the Combined Word Parts

Identify and combine parts

Isolate and spell parts

STEP 3
Work with the Whole Word

Divide into syllables

Spell parts in sequence

STEP 4
Work with Words in Context

Read sentences for meaning

Spell words in sentences

STEP 5
Increase Reading and Spelling Accuracy and Monitor Progress

Read selected words with 90% accuracy

Spell starred words with 90% accura[cy]

STEP 6

Build Reading Proficiency and Monitor Progress

Spontaneous Writing

4

STEP 4. Work with Words in Context

This step provides an opportunity for students to apply their coding skills by using the words in context. Worksheets on vocabulary encourage them to learn word meanings from context as well as to develop dictionary skills. Reading and spelling sentences that emphasize the specific phonic element in each list are also part of this step.

STEP 5. Increase Reading and Spelling Accuracy and Monitor Progress

Students who have successfully completed Steps 1 through 4 are ready for a skill check on reading and spelling. Randomly select ten words from the list for the reading skill check. Ten starred words from the list can be dictated to test spelling accuracy. Skill checks should be repeated until students have achieved 90 percent accuracy or better.

The columns of many of the lists are organized according to vowel sound, prefix, or suffix. Some students may find it less frustrating to read *down* the columns initially, focusing on one pattern at a time. Subsequently, they can read the list by rows, alternating the word patterns.

Have your students record their progress in reading and spelling accuracy on the Accuracy Checklists. A copy of the Accuracy Checklist is provided on page 59 and in the student's workbook. Reading and spelling accuracy scores should be recorded to the right of the Check Test Scores column. These scores can be written as fractions: number correct over number attempted. The date when an accuracy check is done should be noted as well. When students have achieved 90 percent accuracy, they can shade in the box to indicate mastery. The sample Accuracy Checklist below demonstrates its use for record keeping.

The Accuracy Checklist is essential for monitoring your students' progress. It not only enables you to make appropriate instructional decisions but also provides valuable feedback to your students that they are, indeed, improving their skills.

ACCURACY CHECKLIST
Megawords 6, Lists 30–33

Student _Sue Smith_

Record accuracy score as a fraction: $\dfrac{\text{\# correct}}{\text{\# attempted}}$

List	Examples	Check Test Scores Date: 4/8		Reading			Spelling		
		Reading	Spelling	4/8			4/10	4/12	4/15
30. Sounds of *ch*, *ph*, and *que*	chronicle orphanage	$\frac{5}{5}$	$\frac{3}{5}$	mastered			$\frac{7}{10}$	$\frac{8}{10}$	$\frac{10}{10}$
31. Soft *c*	necessary anticipate			4/10	4/12		4/17	4/19	4/22
		$\frac{3}{5}$	$\frac{2}{5}$	$\frac{7}{10}$	$\frac{9}{10}$		$\frac{5}{10}$	$\frac{7}{10}$	$\frac{9}{10}$

STEP 6. Build Reading Proficiency, Monitor Progress, and Encourage Spontaneous Writing

Research indicates that automaticity of decoding skills facilitates reading comprehension and is often a prerequisite to the more complex comprehension skills of reasoning and inference.[1] Students' skills must be automatic (proficient) before they can comprehend a passage or progress to more difficult skills. Thus, once students have demonstrated that they can read the word lists untimed with 90 percent accuracy, they should work on increasing their reading speed by doing frequent rate timings. In our experience, repeated practice and drill are more effective than direct instruction for building proficiency.

Use a stopwatch or second hand to time students as they read the list for a minute. A warm-up timing can be used for practice before doing a second, official, timing. If students finish the list in less than a minute, they should return to the beginning and continue to read until the time is up. Progress is then recorded on the Proficiency Graph, indicating the number of words read correctly in a minute as well as the number of errors. A goal of forty-five to fifty words per minute with two or fewer errors on two of three consecutive days is realistic for most students. This goal can certainly be adjusted for individuals. A sample Proficiency Graph is on page 7. A blank Proficiency Graph is on page 60 and at the back of the student's workbook.

Giving students sufficient practice in spelling words helps the spelling process become automatic. They are then able to concentrate on the content of what they want to express in writing. Their ultimate goal is being able to use correctly spelled words to convey their ideas. Although worksheets on written expression are not included in this program, you should encourage your students to spell the newly learned words in their written work. Creative writing assignments in which students try to include as many words as possible from a given list will provide such an opportunity.

ANALYSIS OF STUDENT PROGRESS FOR DECISION MAKING

Once students have attained 90 percent accuracy in reading words and are working to increase their reading proficiency, instruction should begin on the concepts of the next word list. This way, they will be learning new skills as they improve others. Typically, reading accuracy will be achieved prior to spelling accuracy. Thus, an individual might be working on spelling with List 2, on reading proficiency with List 3, and on reading accuracy with List 4. When you introduce new concepts, include the spelling tasks even if the students are still working to achieve spelling mastery on earlier lists.

If students are not achieving accuracy or proficiency goals, a teaching intervention is necessary. If a student's reading and/or spelling accuracy is not improving, more drill should be done on the learning steps. You can make up games and other creative activities to work on the necessary concepts. Error analysis can help pinpoint the areas of concern. For example, review of a student's mistakes in spelling might reveal difficulty in spelling a specific schwa ending pattern such as -al or -on. You can then provide the necessary drill to remedy the problem.

Lack of progress in reading proficiency also demands attention. If students are making more than four errors on timed readings, discontinue timing them and focus your instruction instead on reading accuracy. Identify and analyze the errors and concentrate your teaching on the specific problem areas. If errors are few but the students are not meeting projected goals, they probably need more practice with the words. Marked improvement can often be made if the students practice the word lists at home. Offering rewards, such as special classroom privileges, for attaining goals is also an effective technique. In some cases, it may be appropriate to lower proficiency goals for students who are having difficulty.

---

[1] E. Haughton, "Aims — Growing and Sharing," in Jordan et al., *Let's Try Doing Something Else Kind of Thing*, Arlington, Va.: The Council for Exceptional Children, 1972.
Barbara Bateman (ed.), *Learning Disorders*, Vol. IV, Seattle, Wash.: Special Child Publications, Inc., 1971.
S.J. Samuels and Patricia Dahl, *A Mastery Based Experimental Program for Teaching Poor Readers High Speed Word Recognition Skills* (Research Report #55), University of Minnesota, 1973.
C. Starlin, "Peers and Precision," *Teaching Exceptional Children*, Vol. 3, No. 3, pp. 129-140, 1971.

PROFICIENCY GRAPH

Student _John Jones_

Goal _50 wpm; 2 errors; 2-3 consecutive days_

●——● Words Read Correctly

×——× Errors

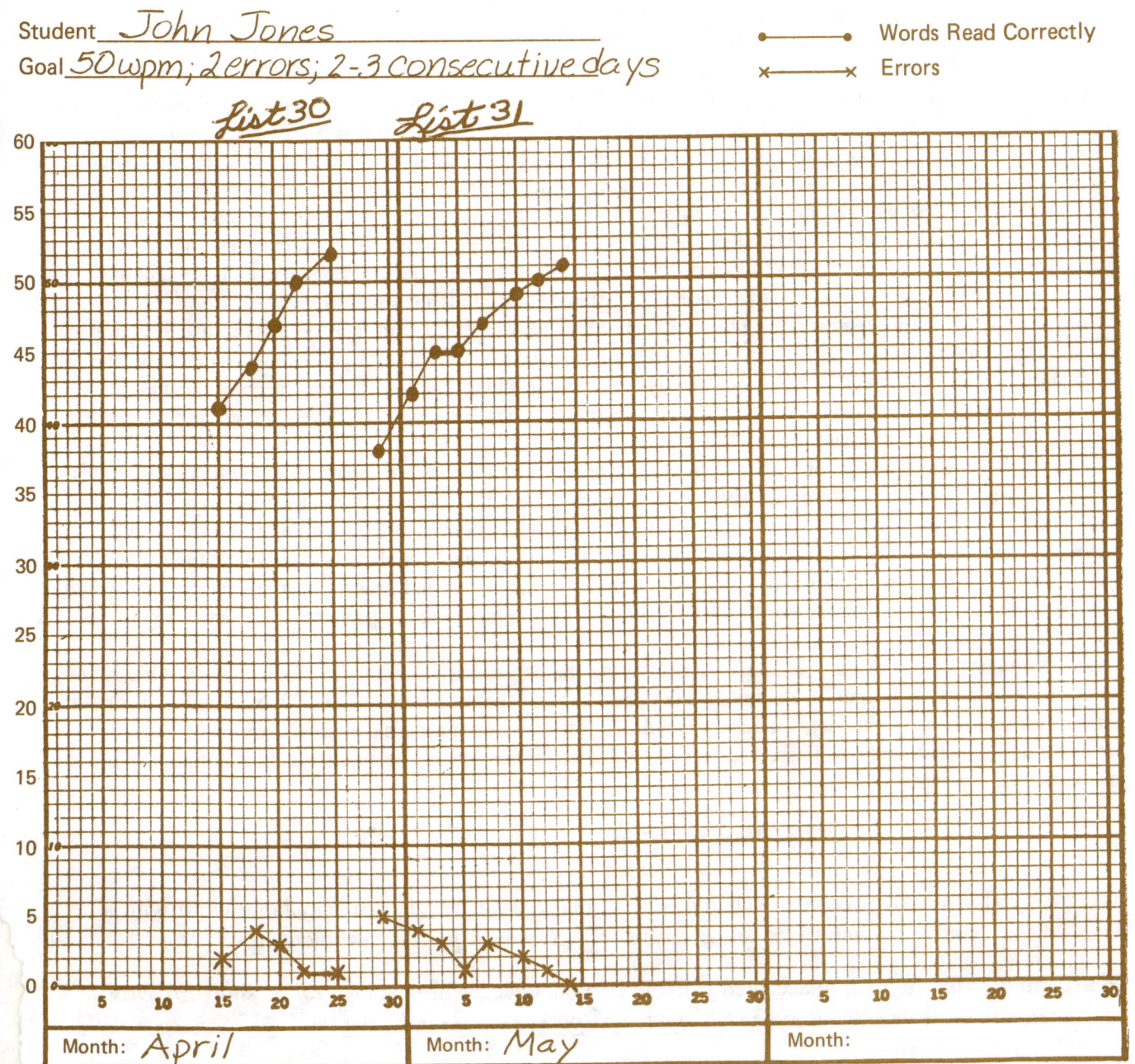

List 30   _List 31_

Month: _April_   Month: _May_   Month: _____

Calendar Days

STUDENT INVOLVEMENT

Student involvement is a *must* throughout all of the learning steps just discussed. Students should be aware of their Check Test results, what they know, and what they need to learn. They should be aware of their progress in both reading and spelling accuracy and proficiency. They should know that the learning steps are divided into small parts to help them reach the ultimate goal of reading and writing fluently. We suggest that the teacher either read To the Student at the beginning of the student's workbook with the students or paraphrase and discuss it.

SPECIAL CONSIDERATIONS FOR *MEGAWORDS 6*

Megawords 6 (Lists 30–33) introduces consonant variations in multisyllabic words. In some ways, Book 6 is the most difficult in the *Megawords* series because students are presented with longer words containing sounds for consonants and consonant combinations different from those with which they are most familiar. In many of the words from Lists 31, 32, and 33, the letter that *follows* a consonant determines the sound that the consonant or preceding vowel has. The soft sounds of *c* (/s/) and *g* (/j/) occur when they are followed by *e, i,* or *y (success, geography)*. The modified long-vowel sounds of the *r*-controlled vowels occur when a vowel or a second *r* and then a vowel follow *(experiment, arrogant)*. In List 30, students must learn alternative sounds for *ch* (/k/ as in *character,* /sh/ as in *mustache),* and *qu* (/k/ as in *conquer). ph* as /f/ *(triumph, photograph)* is also introduced. These patterns may not be familiar to many students as they are not often found in one-syllable words. To help students learn these new sound-symbol relationships, Step 1 activities, Work with the Isolated Word Parts, are essential. Worksheets provide drill on these associations. You should be cautious about proceeding to Step 2 until the students have mastered the sounds in isolation.

Some of the words in *Megawords 6* may not be familiar to students. Encourage students to use a dictionary to look up the definitions of unfamiliar words. In addition, we recommend that you follow Step 4 worksheets, Work with Words in Context, with an oral review of new vocabulary words. Students acquire meaningful vocabulary best when they use words in a variety of contexts. You may wish to devise games and other creative activities to supplement the worksheets.

Since *Megawords 6* focuses on rather difficult consonant variations, accent patterns and syllabication rules are not stressed. Common patterns are shown when relevant, but it is more important for students to concentrate on the consonant variations. The words in Book 6 are much more varied in nature than those in the previous books. Their only commonality might be a soft *c* and frequently only a few words fit the same accent pattern or syllabication rule. Mentioning too many syllabication and accent rules and exceptions would only be confusing. It is often simpler to train students to try the most logical pronunciation, and if that does not work, to try another.

Drill cards or flash cards can be helpful in presenting the consonant variations in *Megawords 6*. One set of cards might have a spelling on one side *(ch, err*V, or *que)* and the pronunciation on the other side (/k/ or /sh/, /air/ or /eer/, or /k/). Another set, for Lists 31 and 32 (soft *c* and *g*), might have isolated syllables such as *gen, cin,* and *ger* that could be flashed to increase a student's rate of reading these syllables commonly found in multisyllabic words.

SUMMARY OF ACCENT PATTERNS

Accented Syllable—An accented syllable is pronounced as if it were a one-syllable word with a clear vowel sound according to its syllabic type *(ac´ tive, com plete´, ser´ vant, loy´ al).*

Unaccented Syllable—An unaccented syllable is pronounced with a schwa /ə/ or short-*i* /ĭ/ vowel sound regardless of its syllabic type *(rib´ bon, op´ po site, in de pen´ dent).*

Accent Patterns—The dark lines and accent marks in this book are accent patterns (__´ __). Each line stands for one syllable. The accent mark shows which syllable is accented. Learning to place the accent on the proper syllable will help you recognize most multisyllabic words. The accent patterns below will help you determine which syllable in a word is accented.

Primary Accent—A strong stress on a syllable in a multisyllabic word.

Secondary Accent—A weaker stress on a syllable in a multisyllabic word.

General Guideline—In two- and three-syllable words, accent the first syllable. Then pronounce the first vowel as if it were a short, long, *r*-controlled, or double-vowel sound in a one-syllable word. If that doesn't make a recognizable word, accent the second syllable, and pronounce the second vowel according to its syllabic type.

Accent Patterns for Two-Syllable Words

1. Accent on the first syllable (__´ __)
   The accent is usually on the first syllable in two-syllable words *(stan´ dard, sis´ ter, dol´ lar).*

2. Accent on the second syllable (__ __´)
   Two-syllable words that have a prefix in the first syllable and a root in the second syllable are usually accented on the second syllable *(ex tend´, con fuse´).*

3. Accent on either the first or second syllable (__´ __ or __ __´)
   If a word can function as both noun and verb, the noun is accented on the prefix *(con´ duct)* and the verb is accented on the root *(con duct´).*

Accent Patterns for Three-Syllable Words

1. Accent on the first syllable (__´ __ __)
   The accent is usually on the first syllable in three-syllable words. The unaccented middle syllable has a schwa sound *(vis´ i tor, char´ ac ter).*

2. Accent on the second syllable (__ __´ __)
   The accent is usually on the second syllable (the root) in words that contain a prefix, root, and suffix *(de stroy´ er, in ven´ tor).*

Accent Patterns for Four-Syllable Words (__ __´ __ __)

1. The accent is usually on the second syllable in four-syllable words *(in tel´ li gence, sig nif´ i cant).*

Special Accent Patterns for Words of Three or More Syllables

Accent patterns for words longer than two syllables are often governed by a specific ending pattern or an unaccented vowel.

1. Accent with the ending *-ic*
   Accent the syllable just before the ending *-ic (fran´ tic, e las´ tic, en er get´ ic, char ac ter is´ tic).*

2. Accent with the ending *-ate* /āt/
   In three-syllable words, the first syllable has a primary accent and *-ate* has a secondary accent *(vi´ o late´).*
   In four-syllable words, the second syllable has a primary accent and *-ate* has a secondary accent *(con grat´ u late´).*

3. Accent with schwa endings
   Schwa endings (and schwa syllables) are never accented. The accent falls on another syllable in the word *(pleas´ ant, in´ no cent, ex ter´ nal, ap pren´ tice).*

4. Accent with the endings *-tion, -sion, -cian*
   Accent the syllable just before the endings *-tion, -sion,* and *-cian (pol lu´ tion, im pres´ sion, ad min is tra´ tion, e lec tri´ cian).*

5. Accent with the ending *-ity* /ĭ tē/.
   Accent the syllable just before the ending *-ity (qual´ i ty, ac tiv´ i ty, per son al´ i ty).*

CHECK TEST: LISTS 30–33

ADMINISTERING THE CHECK TEST

The Check Test informally assesses a student's ability to read and spell words that follow the patterns presented in *Megawords 6*. Although the reading test must be administered individually, the spelling test can be administered to a group.

To test reading, give the student the Student's Reading Copy[1] and instruct him or her to read down the columns. Use the Examiner's Recording Form[2] to note errors and mark the number correct. Enough space is provided after each word to write the student's responses so that errors can be analyzed later.

To test spelling, give the students blank paper and tell them to number from one to five, four times. Dictate the following words to assess their ability to spell frequently used words that follow the patterns presented in *Megawords 6*.

30. Sounds of *ch, ph,* and *que*
1. anchor
2. Chicago
3. orphanage
4. chemical
5. antique

31. Soft *c*
1. receive
2. vaccinate
3. exercise
4. ceiling
5. society

32. Soft *g*
1. general
2. imagine
3. energy
4. religion
5. tragedy

33. V-*r*-V Combinations
1. errand
2. cereal
3. miracle
4. figure
5. marriage

Share the test results with your students so that they become aware of the specific word patterns that they need to learn or review. Be sure constantly to reassess the students' skills as you work with them. Often you will discover strengths or weaknesses that were not revealed in the Check Test results.

If a student misses the first two words of a group and it is apparent that the words are too difficult, discontinue testing in that group. Remember that the purpose of the Check Test is simply to identify specific skill deficits and to determine a starting point for instruction. Do not unnecessarily frustrate the student. In some cases, you may wish to administer the Check Test in sections as the students progress through the book rather than in one sitting.

INTERPRETING RESULTS AND PLANNING INSTRUCTION

Record the students' Check Test results on the Accuracy Checklists. A blank Accuracy Checklist is provided on page 59 and at the back of the student's workbook. Record section scores in reading and spelling as a fraction, writing the number read or spelled correctly over the number five. Refer to the sample Accuracy Checklist on page 5.

By examining the Check Test Scores column, it should be readily apparent which list a student should begin work on. If a student reads and spells all words from a particular section correctly, instruction on the corresponding list is not necessary and it can be marked "mastered." In this case, the student can immedi-

---

[1]The Student's Reading Copy is on page 63. It may be removed and inserted in a plastic cover.

[2]An Examiner's Recording Form appears on page 61 and at the end of each student's workbook. Remove the student's form for the Check Test and keep it for your files. One side can be used for a pretest and the other, for a posttest.

ately begin to build reading proficiency on that list (Step 6). If a student indicates mastery in reading but not in spelling, proceed through the learning steps that focus on the spelling tasks. If a student scores 4/5 for a given list, begin instruction at Step 5, working to increase accuracy. The accuracy check will reveal whether additional instruction on Steps 1 through 4 will be necessary. Obviously a student who reads or spells fewer than three words correctly will require more instructional time than a student who has nearly mastered that list.

LIST 30: SOUNDS OF *ch*, *ph*, AND *que*

ch = /k/ (Greek)	*ch* = /k/ (Greek)	*ch* = /sh/ (French)	*ph* = /f/ (Greek)	*ph* = /f/ (Greek)	*que* = /k/ (French)
anchor	* orchestra	* machine	dolphin	autograph	* conquer
chemist	psychic	brochure	* telephone	phonograph	antique
* stomach	aching	charades	* phonics	telegraph	opaque
echo	chlorine	mustache	* nephew	paragraph	* technique
* Christmas	chaos	chandelier	* orphan	sophomore	oblique
scholar	charisma	champagne	phantom	* physical	critique
* schedule	chronicle	chauffeur	phosphate	Philadelphia	physique
chorus	christen	chivalry	* alphabet	phony	grotesque
* character	monarch	chauvinist	pamphlet	philodendron	picturesque
architect	psychology	chiffon	Phyllis	* elephant	etiquette
* mechanical	psychiatry	chevron	* Phillip	symphony	boutique
* technical	schooner	chateau	atmosphere	catastrophe	* unique
synchronize	chaotic	* Chicago	orphanage	microphone	
orchid	archeology	chagrin	* triumph	physicist	*qu* = /k/
Christopher	chemical	nonchalant	phenomenon	photocopy	* liquor
chronic	melancholy	pistachio	* pharmacy	decipher	mosquito
chrysalis	cholera	echelon	philosophy	physician	
cholesterol	chrysanthemum	chamois	photograph	apostrophe	
chronological	Christian	chalet	pheasant	Philippines	
choreography					

*Practical spelling words. The teacher and student should decide together how many of these words the student will be responsible for spelling.

12

CONCEPTS

Introduce:

Consonant Variations — Sometimes when words come from a foreign language, the consonant combinations make a different sound than one would expect.

• *ch* as /k/ — In words of Greek origin, *ch* says /k/ as in *anchor* and *chemical*.

• *ch* as /sh/ — In words of French origin, *ch* says /sh/ as in *Chicago* and *machine*.

• *ph* as /f/ — In words of Greek origin, *ph* says /f/ as in *photo* and *dolphin*.

• *que* as /k/ — In words of French origin, *que* says /k/. It is usually found at the end of words as in *conquer* and *picturesque*. *-ique* says /ēk/ as in *antique* in words of French origin. The rare *qu* as /k/ in *liquor* and *mosquito* is also included here. It may be necessary to teach your students the pronunciation of French words such as *champagne*, *chauffeur*, *chateau*, *chamois*, and *chalet*.

Review:

ch as /ch/ — The most common sound of *ch* in English words is /ch/ as in *chapter* and *archery*.

tch as /ch/ — *tch* is the spelling of the /ch/ sound at the end of a closed syllable after a short vowel as in *matching* and *catcher*.

sh as /sh/ — The most common spelling of the /sh/ sound in English words is *sh* as in *shadow* and *mashing*.

f as /f/ — The most common spelling of the /f/ sound in English words is *f* as in *feather* and *filter*.

Digraphs — You may wish to review the concept of a digraph and the more common digraphs (*ch*, *sh*, *wh*, *th*).

Spelling of /k/ — The /k/ sound can be spelled in five ways as the chart illustrates. The spellings are listed in order of frequency.

Use *c*	• before vowels *a, o,* and *u* • before consonants • at the end of words of two or more syllables	*campus, college, curing* *clatter, crisis* *shellac, traffic, Atlantic, fantastic*
Use *k*	• before *i, e,* and *y*	*kitchen, monkey, risky*
Use *ck*	• at the end of a syllable after a short vowel	*black, trick, hockey, stocking*
Use *que*	• in words of French origin—usually at the end	*antique, picturesque*
Use *ch*	• in words of Greek origin	*chorus, orchid*

You may wish to review the three most common spellings of the /k/ sound: *c, k,* and *ck. ch* and *que* as /k/ are found in more specialized words that are not used frequently in writing. Since no rule governs when to use *ch* or *que* in spelling the /k/ sound, words must be memorized.

LEARNING STEPS

STEP 1. Work with the Isolated Word Parts

Reading — The students will correctly pronounce the following sounds, giving more than one sound if appropriate.

Spelling	Sound	Use
ch	/ch/	most common
	/k/	in words of Greek origin
	/sh/	in words of French origin
ph	/f/	in words of Greek origin
que	/k/	in words of French origin

(See Worksheet 30–A.)

Refer to Special Considerations on page 8 for a description of reading drill card techniques.

Spelling — The students will write the various spellings for the following sounds:

/f/ spelled *f* (usually) and *ph* (Greek)

/sh/ spelled *sh* (usually) and *ch* (French)

/k/ spelled *k, c,* or *ck* (usually), *ch* (Greek), and *que* (French)

(See Worksheet 30–B.)

Refer to Special Considerations on page 8 for a description of spelling drill card techniques.

STEP 2. Work with the Combined Word Parts

Reading — The students will pronounce detached syllables and then combine them to read a whole word. (See Worksheet 30–C.)

Spelling — The students will isolate, pronounce, and spell syllables heard in dictated words. (See Worksheet 30–D.)

Dictate slowly the following words for Worksheet 30–D. Make certain that the students repeat the word *(character)*, isolate the missing syllables *(ac, ter)*, and say them aloud while spelling.

ch = /k/ 1. an<u>ch</u>or   2. e<u>ch</u>o   3. chara<u>c</u>ter   4. te<u>ch</u>nical   5. <u>ch</u>emical
       6. me<u>ch</u>anical

ph = /f/ 7. dol<u>ph</u>in   8. <u>ph</u>otogra<u>ph</u>   9. <u>Ph</u>iladelphia 10. tele<u>ph</u>one 11. <u>ph</u>armacy

ch = /sh/ 12. <u>Ch</u>icago   13. ma<u>ch</u>ine   14. musta<u>ch</u>e   15. bro<u>ch</u>ure   16. <u>ch</u>ivalry

que = /k/ 17. con<u>quer</u>   18. opa<u>que</u>   19. pictures<u>que</u> 20. techni<u>que</u> 21. uni<u>que</u>
       22. grotes<u>que</u>

STEP 3. Work with the Whole Word

Reading — The students will syllabify, read, and classify List 30 words. (See Worksheets 30–E and 30–F.)

Spelling — The students will practice spelling words from List 30. (See Worksheets 30–G and 30–H.)

STEP 4. Work with Words in Context

Meaning — The students will use List 30 words in definitions and in context. (See Worksheets 30–I, 30–J, and 30–K.)

Reading and Spelling — The students will read and write sentences that contain List 30 words. (See Worksheet 30–L.)

Note: Any words that exemplify the principles of the word list may be circled.

STEP 5. Increase Reading and Spelling Accuracy and Monitor Progress

Reading — The students will read ten randomly selected words from List 30 with 90 percent accuracy. Record their progress on the Accuracy Checklists.

Spelling — The students will spell from dictation ten practical spelling words from List 30 with 90 percent accuracy. Record their progress on the Accuracy Checklists.

STEP 6. Build Reading Proficiency, Monitor Progress, and Encourage Spontaneous Writing

Record students' progress on the Proficiency Graphs.

LIST 31: SOFT c

concept	* center	* city	* circle	recede
* accept	census	* civic	* circus	* faucet
* except	* license	* cigar	circuit	* citric
* receive	censor	* recipe	* circumstance	deficit
deceive	* central	* accident	ulcer	placid
* success	descend	* incident	* cancer	rancid
access	* accent	* citizen	* concern	acid
* princess	* century	* principal	* certain	deceitful
* recess	* recent	* icicle	* concert	* receipt
* process	* concentrate	anticipate	* grocery	decisive
* necessary	centimeter	* civilized	* certificate	* society
recession	accentuate	taciturn	* pencil	* cemetery
ancestor	centipede	reciprocate	stencil	* cement
* necessity	descendant	certainly	council	* medicine
* proceed	concentration	acetate	facilitate	cinnamon
* exceed	cinder	* vaccinate	* cancel	incinerate
* succeed	* fascinated	* fancy	* celery	succinct
Cincinnati	Cyprus	frequency	* circular	cylinder
rescinded	* cellar	* mercy	* excellent	* cereal
irascible	* vacancy	* decide	* celebrate	* sincere
* exercise	* emergency	* cider	accelerator	conceal
* criticize	* democracy	homicide	celestial	* ceiling
recite	spicy	* December	* bicycle	* decision
cyclone	* accuracy	* cigarette	cymbal	* civilization

*Practical spelling words. The teacher and student should decide together how many of these words the student will be responsible for spelling.

CONCEPTS

Introduce:

Soft-c Rule — When *c* is followed by *e, i,* or *y,* it has its soft sound, /s/, as in *face, city,* and *cycle*. Followed by any other letter, it has its hard sound, /k/, as in *cat, crop, cute,* and *coat*.

Students should be somewhat familiar with the soft sound of *c* in a number of one-syllable, silent-*e* words that end in *ce (race, nice, place)*. Many students experience difficulty applying this rule to multisyllabic words because there are few one-syllable words in which *c* precedes *e, i,* or *y* at the beginning or in the middle of a word. Furthermore, the students must now apply this rule to isolated syllables rather than meaningful words. Frequent drill with the isolated parts will help the students become so familiar with the rule that they will be able to apply it automatically. Drill cards can be very helpful. To begin, students should be able to state the Soft-*c* Rule.

Review:

Vowel Sounds of y — *y* is a consonant only when it appears at the beginning of a word or syllable *(yellow, yesterday, beyond)*. In any other position, it is a vowel. As a vowel it has three possible sounds: /ē/ as in *happy*, /ī/ as in *cycle*, or /ĭ/ as in *myth*. Refer to *Megawords 5*, List 29, for a further description of the vowel sounds of *y*.

It is helpful for students to learn the three sounds of *cy*:
- *cy* says /sē/ as in *fancy*.
- *cy* says /sī/ as in *cyclone*.
- *cy* says /sĭ/ as in *cymbal*.

Worksheet 31–H provides practice with the *cy* combination.

LEARNING STEPS

STEP 1. Work with the Isolated Word Parts

Reading — The students will identify letter combinations in which *c* says /s/ and pronounce syllables that contain the soft-*c* sound. (See Worksheets 31–A and 31–B.)

The syllables included on Worksheets 31–A and 31–B are taken directly from List 31 words. Thus, students are presented with the letter combinations they need for pronouncing soft-*c*, multisyllabic words.

Spelling — The students will spell dictated syllables in which *c* is used to spell the /s/ sound. (See Worksheet 31–C.)

Dictate the following syllables for the top of Worksheet 31–C.

1. cip	2. cite	3. cept	4. cel	5. cin
6. cen	7. ceed	8. cess	9. cit	10. cide

Dictate slowly the following words for the bottom of Worksheet 31–C. Stress the first syllable of each word.

1. cider	2. cigarette	3. cemetery	4. cement	5. celebrate
6. citizen	7. circle	8. civilization		

STEP 2. Work with the Combined Word Parts

Reading— The students will pronounce detached syllables and then combine them to read a whole word. (See Worksheet 31-D.)

Spelling— The students will practice spelling syllables heard in soft-*c*, multisyllabic words. (See Worksheets 31-E, 31-F, 31-G, and 31-H.)

Dictate the following words for Worksheet 31–E. Make certain that the students repeat the word *(infancy)*, isolate the missing syllables *(in, cy)*, and say them aloud while spelling.

1. center	2. cancel	3. circle	4. infancy	5. census
6. ulcer	7. concern	8. successful	9. except	10. grocery
11. accelerator	12. Cincinnati	13. fascinate	14. deficit	15. celebrate
16. certificate				

STEP 3. Work with the Whole Word

Reading — The students will syllabify soft-*c*, multisyllabic words and pronounce them. (See Worksheets 31–I, 31–J, 31–K, 31–L, and 31–M.)

Spelling — The students will spell practical spelling words from List 31. (See Worksheet 31–N.)

Dictate the following practical spelling words for Worksheet 31–N, slightly stressing the soft-*c* syllables. You may need to go slowly and help students get started on this worksheet.

1. center	2. circus	3. success	4. accept	5. recipe
6. cereal	7. vacancy	8. concert	9. celebrate	10. century
11. accident	12. except	13. decide	14. emergency	15. circle
16. license	17. receive	18. exercise	19. excellent	20. sincere
21. citizen	22. recess	23. society	24. concentrate	25. certain

STEP 4. Work with Words in Context

Meaning — The students will use List 31 words in definitions and in context. (See Worksheets 31–O, 31–P, and 31–Q.)

Reading and Spelling — The students will read and write sentences that contain List 31 words. (See Worksheet 31–R.)

Note: Any words that exemplify the principles of the word list may be circled.

STEP 5. Increase Reading and Spelling Accuracy and Monitor Progress

Reading — The students will read ten randomly selected words from List 31 with 90 percent accuracy. Record their progress on the Accuracy Checklists.

Spelling — The students will spell from dictation ten practical spelling words from List 31 with 90 percent accuracy. Record their progress on the Accuracy Checklists.

STEP 6. Build Reading Proficiency, Monitor Progress, and Encourage Spontaneous Writing

Record students' progress on the Proficiency Graphs.

LIST 32: SOFT *g*

*gentle	ginger	*magic	indulge
*agent	*margin	*tragic	*college
urgent	*engine	logic	submerge
legend	origin	*angel	impinge
gently	*imagine	gelatin	enrage
pungent	*original	vigil	*engagement
gentry	wager	gesture	infringe
tangent	*German	*suggest	indulgent
gender	*messenger	*digestion	stingy
genuine	*passenger	congestion	clergy
*emergency	exaggerate	rigid	dingy
*general	*dangerous	*register	*energy
*generation	plunger	tangible	allergy
contingency	*giraffe	longitude	gypsum
germicide	*gigantic	eligible	Gypsy
astringent	*giant	regiment	*gymnastics
ingenuity	*genius	*legislate	*Egypt
urgency	genie	legible	*gymnasium
gemstone	*geography	pugilist	gyroscope
*tragedy	geometry	*region	*surgeon
energetic	*vegetable	*religion	*pigeon
longevity	geology	fugitive	gyrate
*gentleman	*generous	Georgia	gesticulate

*Practical spelling words. The teacher and student should decide together how many of these words the student will be responsible for spelling.

CONCEPTS

Introduce:

Soft-g Rule — When *g* is followed by *e, i,* or *y*, it usually has its soft sound, /j/, as in *cage, giant,* and *gym*. Followed by any other letter, it has its hard sound, /g/, as in *goat, grin,* and *gas*.

Unlike the Soft-*c* Rule, there are some common exceptions to the Soft-*g* Rule. Thus, it is important for students to include the word *usually* when reciting the Soft-*g* Rule: When *g* is followed by *e, i,* or *y*, it usually has its soft sound, /j/. The common exceptions will be familiar to most students. They are:

get	girl	begin	gear	anger
gift	give	gig	geese	finger
hunger	girdle	giddy	nugget	gingham

The Soft-*g* Rule does not apply when the suffixes *-ing* and *-er* are attached to a root ending in *g*, such as *longer, bigger, singing,* or *bringing*.

Students should be somewhat familiar with the soft sound of *g* in a number of one-syllable, silent-*e* words that end in *ge* (*cage, page*) and one-syllable words that end in *dge* (*badge, bridge*). As with the soft-*c* sound, students may experience difficulty applying the Soft-*g* Rule to sound out multisyllabic words. To ease this transition, frequent drill is needed on the isolated syllables that contain the soft-*g* sound. Do not proceed until students have clearly mastered Step 1.

Review:

Soft-c Rule — See explanation in List 31. Point out to students that the rule for the soft sound of *g* is the same as for the soft sound of *c*.

Vowel Sounds of y — *y* is a consonant only when it appears at the beginning of a word or syllable (*yellow, yesterday, beyond*). In any other position it has one of three vowel sounds: /ē/ as in *happy*, /ī/ as in *cycle*, or /ĭ/ as in *myth*.

The vowel *y* in multisyllabic words is treated as a separate element in *Megawords 5*, List 29. It is helpful for students to learn the three sounds of *gy*:

- *gy* says /gē/ as in *stingy*.
- *gy* says /gī/ as in *gyrate*.
- *gy* says /gĭ/ as in *Gypsy*.

Worksheet 32–G provides practice with the *gy* combination.

LEARNING STEPS

STEP 1. Work with the Isolated Word Parts

Reading — The students will identify letter combinations in which *g* says /j/ and pronounce syllables that contain the soft-*g* sound. (See Worksheets 32–A and 32–B.)

The syllables included in Worksheets 32–A and 32–B are taken directly from List 32 words. Thus, students are presented with the letter combinations they need for pronouncing soft-*g*, multisyllabic words.

Spelling — The students will spell dictated syllables in which *g* is used to spell the /j/ sound. (See Worksheet 32–C.)

Dictate the following syllables for the top of Worksheet 32–C.

1. gen	2. ger	3. gel	4. gi (/jī/)	5. gic
6. gin	7. gest	8. gem		

Dictate slowly the following words for the bottom of Worksheet 32–C. Stress the first syllable of each word.

1. geometry	2. gemstone	3. gesture	4. gentle	5. germicide
6. gelatin	7. ginger	8. Gypsy		

STEP 2. Work with the Combined Word Parts

Reading — The students will pronounce detached syllables and then combine them to read a whole word. (See Worksheet 32–D.)

Spelling — The students will practice spelling syllables heard in soft-*g*, multisyllabic words. (See Worksheets 32–E, 32–F, and 32–G.)

Dictate the following words for Worksheet 32–E. Make certain that the students repeat the word (*allergy*), isolate the missing syllables (*al, gy*), and say them aloud while spelling.

1. gentle	2. Gypsy	3. allergy	4. suggestion	5. passenger
6. logic	7. urgent	8. margin	9. gigantic	10. submerge
11. gelatin	12. legislate	13. dangerous	14. giant	15. genuine
16. tragedy				

STEP 3. Work with the Whole Word

Reading — The students will syllabify soft-*g*, multisyllabic words and pronounce them. (See Worksheets 32–H, 32–I, and 32–J.)

Spelling — The students will practice spelling soft-*g* words. (See Worksheets 32–K and 32–L.)

Dictate the following practical spelling words for Worksheet 32–L, slightly stressing the soft-*g* syllables.

1. magic	2. gentle	3. digestion	4. surgeon	5. energy
6. German	7. tragic	8. general	9. dangerous	10. generous
11. register	12. giant	13. angel	14. gigantic	15. suggest
16. passenger				

STEP 4. Work with Words in Context

Meaning — The students will use List 32 words in definitions and in context. (See Worksheets 32–M and 32–N.)

Reading and Spelling — The students will read and write sentences that contain List 32 words. (See Worksheet 32–O.)

Note: Any words that exemplify the principles of the word list may be circled.

STEP 5. Increase Reading and Spelling Accuracy and Monitor Progress

Reading — The students will read ten randomly selected words from List 32 with 90 percent accuracy. Record their progress on the Accuracy Checklists.

Spelling — The students will spell from dictation ten practical spelling words from List 32 with 90 percent accuracy. Record their progress on the Accuracy Checklists.

STEP 6. Build Reading Proficiency, Monitor Progress, and Encourage Spontaneous Writing

Record students' progress on the Proficiency Graphs.

LIST 33: VOWEL-r-VOWEL COMBINATIONS

arV = /air/	arrV = /air/	erV, errV = /air/	erV, errV = /air/	irV, irrV = /eer/	ary = /air ē/
* care	* carrot	* there	* errand	* mirror	* vary
* scare	carry	sheriff	prosperity	* spirit	wary
Harold	* parrot	* terrible	geriatric	* miracle	* January
Paris	* arrow	herring	inherit	virile	* February
Sarah	marry	terror	veritable	* irritate	primary
* charity	* narrow	* cherry	* America	irresistible	secondary
* parent	* sparrow	* merry	* territory	conspiracy	* dictionary
parakeet	* barrel	peril	erudite	irritable	* vocabulary
parasite	barricade	perish		* irrigate	preliminary
* parallel	barracuda	* merit	erV = /eer/	irregular	* temporary
* paragraph	* marriage	* stereo	* here	spiritual	mercenary
paradise	carriage	* experiment	* hero	irrational	capillary
variable	arrogant	kerosene	* zero	irresponsible	corollary
baritone	narrative	hysterical	* cereal	irascible	* ordinary
caravan		terrace	* severe	* irrigation	sanitary
* character		therapy	* period	miraculous	* secretary
parachute		* clerical	revere		honorary
disparity		* ceremony	* merely	urV = /yoor/	coronary
charitable		heroin	* sincere	* secure	military
barometric		imperative	* series	* security	legendary
* apparent		interrogate	* experience	mercury	evolutionary
barbarian		derivation	managerial	fury	revolutionary
* comparison		sterilize	interference	purity	tributary
		heritage	* cafeteria	* accuracy	discretionary
		stereotype	Erie	* figure	dignitary
		verify	persevere	urine	
		* error	* interfere	bureau	

*Practical spelling words. The teacher and student should decide together how many of these words the student will be responsible for spelling.

CONCEPTS

Introduce:

Vowel-r-Vowel (VrV) Pattern — If an accented vowel-r combination is followed by a vowel, the first vowel has a modified long-vowel sound. These sounds must be memorized.

- *ar*V says /air/ as in *care*.
- *ir*V says /eer/ as in *spirit*.
- *er*V says /eer/ as in *here* and /air/ as in *there*.
- *ur*V says /yoor/ as in *cure*.

Vowel-r-r-Vowel (VrrV) Pattern — The VrV sound patterns also apply when the vowels *a, e,* and *i* are followed by two *r*s and a vowel.

- *arr*V says /air/ as in *carry*.
- *err*V says /air/ as in *berry*.
- *irr*V says /eer/ as in *mirror*.

Regional differences in dialect may suggest different sounds from those listed here. If so, teach what is appropriate for your locale.

The VrV pattern occurs in a few two-syllable words but is most frequently found in three- and four-syllable words. It is typically a difficult generalization for students to apply as it requires their learning a new sound correspondence for the vowel-r combination. It may help to introduce these sounds with drill cards as follows: first, introduce the *ar*V card as /air/, placing it to the left. Next, introduce the *ir*V card as /eer/, placing it to the right. Finally, introduce the *er*V card as both /air/ and /eer/, placing it between the *ar*V and the *ir*V cards. The *2* in the upper right-hand corner indicates that *er*V has two sounds. The *ur*V drill card can be introduced as /yoor/.

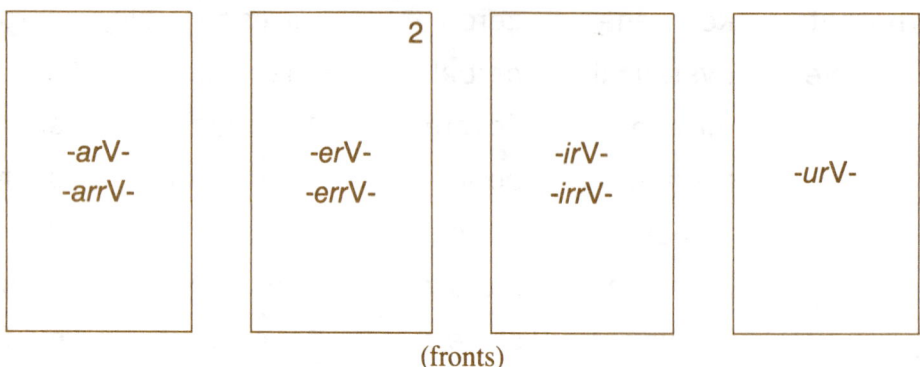

(fronts)

On the backs, the sounds and common key words can be written.

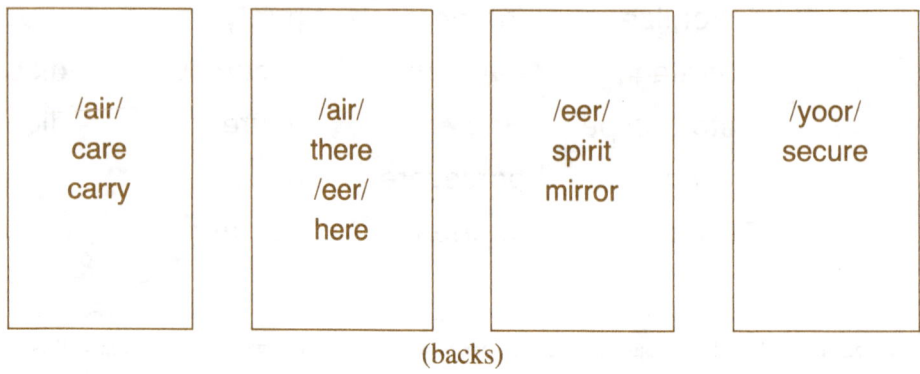

(backs)

22

Once students have mastered the sound cards in this position, the cards can be mixed up for further drill.

Owing to the complexity of the VrV combinations, students should have their own drill cards. If they have difficulty memorizing the isolated sounds on the drill cards, you may want to introduce these sounds in context through the patterned practice provided in the worksheets.

If the VrV pattern is unaccented, the vowel-r combination sounds like /er/ or /ə/. Since this occurs in relatively few words, we recommend that you *not* teach this auxiliary generalization. For your reference, some words that contain the unaccented VrV pattern are listed below.

meridian	perimeter	terrific	directory	paralysis
generous	several	separate	ferocity	camera
funeral				opera

urV is described as sounding like /yoor/ in *Megawords 6*. While /yu(ə)r/ may be technically more correct, /yoor/ seems more easily understandable for students with learning problems. Again, regional differences in dialect may suggest a slightly different pronunciation in some areas.

Review:

r-Controlled Syllable (Vr) — An r-controlled syllable contains a vowel followed by r, which modifies the vowel sound as follows:

ar says /ar/ as in *car*.
ir says /er/ as in *bird*.
ur says /er/ as in *church*. } These all have the same sound: /er/.
er says /er/ as in *fern*.
or says /or/ as in *fort*.

The sound pattern above applies when a vowel-r combination is followed by a consonant or ends a word *(murder, permit, carpenter)*. Students should have already mastered this concept in *Megawords 1,* List 4.

LEARNING STEPS

STEP 1. Work with the Isolated Word Parts

Reading — The students will identify words in which the vowel-r combination is followed by a vowel. (See Worksheet 33–A.)

Spelling — The students will spell dictated syllables that contain the /eer/, /air/, and /yoor/ sounds of the VrV combinations. (See Worksheet 33–B.)

Dictate the following syllables and sample words for Worksheet 33–B. Students may need to be shown how to do the first few syllables.

Part 1

1. par as in *parent*	2. mir as in *miracle*	3. cur as in *security*
4. spir as in *spirit*	5. var as in *variable*	6. bar as in *baritone*
7. pur as in *purity*	8. vir as in *virile*	9. char as in *charity*
10. bur as in *bureau*	11. har as in *Harold*	12. fur as in *furious*

Part 2

1. her as in *here*	2. ser as in *series*	3. ter as in *cafeteria*
4. per as in *experience*	5. mer as in *merely*	6. fer as in *interference*

Part 3

1. ther as in *therapy*	2. der as in *derivation*	3. mer as in *merit*
4. per as in *experiment*	5. her as in *heritage*	6. ster as in *hysterical*
7. cler as in *clerical*	8. ver as in *verify*	

Point out that these syllables, if read in isolation, would have different sounds. Emphasize that the purpose of this exercise is to practice ways to spell these sounds in multisyllabic words.

STEP 2. Work with the Combined Word Parts

Reading — The students will pronounce detached syllables and combine them to read a whole word. (See Worksheets 33–C and 33–D.)

Spelling — The students will practice spelling syllables heard in V*r*V combination words. (See Worksheets 33–E, 33–F, and 33–G.)

Dictate the following words for Worksheet 33–E. Make certain that the students repeat the word (*irregular*), isolate the missing syllabes *(ir, lar),* and say them aloud while spelling.

1. parent	2. mirror	3. carrot	4. security	5. charity
6. miracle	7. narrow	8. irregular	9. accuracy	10. paragraph
11. character	12. irresistible			

STEP 3. Work with the Whole Word

Reading — The students will syllabify V*r*V combination words and pronounce them. (See Worksheets 33–H, 33–I, and 33–J.)

The instruction to divide after *r* is given to simplify syllabication for the students. In some words, dictionaries show division *before* the *r*, as in *geriatric*. A student's ability to pronounce and spell the words is more important than technically correct syllabication.

Spelling — The students will practice spelling V*r*V combination words. (See Worksheets 33–K, 33–L, 33–M, and 33–N.)

Dictate the following practical spelling words for Worksheet 33–N. This exercise is quite difficult. You may need to lead students through it step by step.

1. arrow	2. secure	3. carrot	4. cereal	5. merry
6. period	7. cafeteria	8. miracle	9. stereo	10. sincere
11. America	12. charity	13. experience	14. irritate	15. terrible
16. character				

STEP 4. Work with Words in Context

Meaning — The students will use List 33 words in definitions and in context. (See Worksheets 33–O, 33–P, and 33–Q.)

Reading and Spelling — The students will read and write sentences that contain List 33 words. (See Worksheet 33–R.)

Note: Any words that exemplify the principles of the word list may be circled.

STEP 5. Increase Reading and Spelling Accuracy and Monitor Progress

Reading — The students will read ten randomly selected words from List 33 with 90 percent accuracy. Record their progress on the Accuracy Checklists.

Notice that the columns of List 33 are organized according to the vowel sounds made by the V*r*V combinations. Students should initially read down the columns focusing on one sound at a time. Subsequently, they should read the list by rows, alternating the vowel sounds.

Spelling — The students will spell from dictation ten practical spelling words from List 33 with 90 percent accuracy. Record their progress on the Accuracy Checklists.

STEP 6. Build Reading Proficiency, Monitor Progress, and Encourage Spontaneous Writing

Record students' progress on the Proficiency Graphs.

REVIEW: LISTS 30–33

chlorine	* license	* magic	* parrot
* stereo	scholar	* grocery	* suggest
* certificate	genuine	* miracle	chateau
rigid	kerosene	* unique	* necessary
pamphlet	* citizen	* gigantic	* parallel
rancid	charades	* temporary	* register
mustache	* character	* legislate	* accuracy
parachute	* cemetery	monarch	* tragedy
* circular	* region	irritable	architect
energetic	* physical	* celebrate	therapy
pheasant	paradise	allergy	cylinder
* icicle	* passenger	brochure	* ceremony
* imagine	ancestor	* figure	chemical
* ordinary	* technique	* accent	exaggerate
sophomore	* error	* gymnastics	* succeed

*Practical spelling words. The teacher and student should decide together how many of these words the student will be responsible for spelling.

LEARNING STEPS

For the Review List, only Steps 5 and 6 are applicable.

STEP 5. Increase Reading and Spelling Accuracy and Monitor Progress

Reading — The students will read ten randomly selected words from the Review List with 90 percent accuracy. Record their progress on the Accuracy Checklists.

Spelling — The students will spell from dictation ten practical spelling words from the Review List with 90 percent accuracy. Record their progress on the Accuracy Checklists.

STEP 6. Build Reading Proficiency, Monitor Progress, and Encourage Spontaneous Writing

Record students' progress on the Proficiency Graphs.

WORKSHEET 30—A

Sometimes when words come from a foreign language, the consonant combinations make a different sound than you would expect.

ch says /k/ as in *mechanic* in words of Greek origin.
ch says /sh/ as in *Chicago* in words of French origin.
ph says /f/ as in *phone* in words of Greek origin.
**que* says /k/ as in *conquer* in words of French origin.

Circle *ch, ph,* and *que* in the words below. Write the sound each consonant combination makes above it. "Gr." after a word means that it is Greek in origin. "Fr." after a word means that it is French in origin. Remember that *ch* says /ch/ in most English words.

/ch/ charter	/k/ technical (Gr.)	/k/ chorus (Gr.)	/sh/ chivalry (Fr.)
/sh/ machine (Fr.)	/sh/ pistachio (Fr.)	/k/ chaos (Gr.)	/sh/ brochure (Fr.)
/f/ atmosphere (Gr.)	/ch/ chapter	/k/ chemical (Gr.)	/k/ unique (Fr.)
/k/ conquer (Fr.)	/f/ dolphin (Gr.)	triumph (Gr.) /f/	/f/ sophomore (Gr.)
/k/ antique (Fr.)	/ch/ chilly	/k/ architect (Gr.)	/ch/ matching
/f/ orphan (Gr.)	/k//k/ technique (Fr.)	/f/ pamphlet (Gr.)	/sh/ champagne (Fr.)
/f/ symphony (Gr.)	/k/ chronic (Gr.)	/k//f/ Christopher (Gr.)	/k/ grotesque (Fr.)

Review: 1. *ch* says /k/, /sh/, and /ch/.
2. *ph* says /f/ in words of Greek origin.
3. *que* says /k/ in words of French origin.

*qu says /k/ in *liquor* and *mosquito.* However, *qu* says /kwə/ in almost all other English words.
-ique says /ēk/ as in *antique* in words of French origin.

2

WORKSHEET 30—B

Spell the words below by choosing the correct spelling for the underlined sound. First, write the spelling above the sound; then write the whole word.

In words of Greek origin:
/k/ is spelled *ch.*
/f/ is spelled *ph.*

In words of French origin:
/sh/ is spelled *ch.*
/k/ is spelled *que.*

ch ankor	__anchor__	ch mashine	__machine__
ph dolfin	__dolphin__	que antk	__antique__
ch orkestra	__orchestra__	que oblik	__oblique__
ch kemical	__chemical__	Ch Shicago	__Chicago__
ph ph foslate	__phosphate__	ch mustashe	__mustache__
ph pamflet	__pamphlet__	ch sharades	__charades__
Ph ph Filadelfia	__Philadelphia__	que corkr	__conquer__
ch korus	__chorus__	ch shampane	__champagne__
ch eko	__echo__	que technik	__technique__
ch psykology	__psychology__	ch shandelier	__chandelier__
ph fotograf	__photograph__	ch broshure	__brochure__

Review: /k/ is spelled __ch__ in words of Greek origin.
/f/ is spelled __ph__ in words of Greek origin.

/sh/ is spelled __ch__ in words of French origin.
/k/ is spelled __que__ in words of French origin.

3

Pronounce and combine the syllables. Then cover the divided word and practice reading the whole word. Underline *ch*, *ph*, or *que* in the whole word.

ch = /k/ (Greek)

an chor	anchor
stom ach	stomach
ech o	echo
cha os	chaos
chlor ine	chlorine
char ac ter	character
ar chi tect	architect
tech ni cal	technical
me chan i cal	mechanical
psy chol o gy	psychology
psy chi a try	psychiatry
mel an chol y	melancholy
chron o log i cal	chronological
cho re og ra phy	choreography

que = /k/ (French)

o paque	opaque
tech nique	technique
phy sique	physique
gro tesque	grotesque
con quer	conquer
li quor	liquor
mos qui to	mosquito
pic tur esque	picturesque

ch = /sh/ (French)

ma chine	machine
cha grin	chagrin
mus tache	mustache
Chi ca go	Chicago
chan de lier	chandelier
chau vin ist	chauvinist
non cha lant	nonchalant
pis ta chi o	pistachio

ph = /f/ (Greek)

dol phin	dolphin
sul phur	sulphur
Phil lip	Phillip
phar ma cy	pharmacy
pho to graph	photograph
at mos phere	atmosphere
tel e phone	telephone
phe nom e non	phenomenon
phi los o phy	philosophy
Phil a del phi a	Philadelphia

4

Your teacher will dictate some words. Sound out each word as you write the missing syllable(s). Then write the whole word, saying it aloud as you spell it.

/k/ = *ch* (Greek)

1. an **chor** — anchor
2. **ech** o — echo
3. char **ac** **ter** — character
4. **tech** ni cal — technical
5. **chemical** — chemical
6. me **chan** i **cal** — mechanical

/f/ = *ph* (Greek)

7. dol **phin** — dolphin
8. **pho** to **graph** — photograph
9. **Phil** a **del** phi a — Philadelphia
10. **tel** e **phone** — telephone
11. **phar** ma **cy** — pharmacy

/sh/ = *ch* (French)

12. **Chi** ca **go** — Chicago
13. ma **chine** — machine
14. **mus** tache — mustache
15. **bro** chure — brochure
16. **chiv** al **ry** — chivalry

/k/ = *que* (French)

17. con **quer** — conquer
18. o **paque** — opaque
19. **pic** tur **esque** — picturesque
20. tech **nique** — technique
21. u **nique** — unique
22. gro **tesque** — grotesque

Review: In *liquor* and *mosquito*, *qu* says / **k** /. However, in almost all other English words *qu* says /kwə/.

5

WORKSHEET 30–E

Write a *k* after the words in which *ch* says /k/.

anchor	k	chlorine	k	charisma	k
cherry	__	chrome	k	cholera	__
ache	k	chimpanzee	__	birches	__
chemist	k	chauvinist	__	chorus	k
echo	k	monarch	k	chapped	__
Chicago	__	schooling	k	chaotic	k
		cholesterol	k	chocolate	__
				chiffon	__

Read the words below. All of them contain the letters *ch*. Divide them into syllables and then write each word under the correct heading.

chicken	orchid	architect
chemist	charter	archery
champagne	champion	Chicago
approach	chalet	French
	machine	schedule
	Christmas	stomach
	chauffeur	cholesterol
	itchy	charades

ch, tch = /ch/	*ch* = /k/ (Greek)	*ch* = /sh/ (French)
chicken	chemist	champagne
approach	orchid	chalet
charter	architect	Chicago
champion	Christmas	machine
archery	schedule	chauffeur
French	stomach	charades
itchy	cholesterol	

Review: *ch* has three sounds. *ch* usually says /ch/.

In words of Greek origin, *ch* says /k/.

In words of French origin, *ch* says /sh/.

WORKSHEET 30–F

Simple syllabication rules do not always work for dividing long words and words of foreign origin. Accent patterns* are also more difficult to determine. The best approach is to try one logical syllabication or accent pattern and if that does not work, to try another.

Write the following words, which fit three common accent patterns, by syllables. Write the accented syllables in the boxes. Underline the Greek or French spelling, and write the sound above it.

(sound written above underlined letters; boxed syllable shown in 【 】)

- *k* — **character:** 【char】 — ac — ter
- *k* — **cholera:** 【chol】 — er — a
- **telephone:** 【tel】 — e — phone *(f)*
- *k* — **orchestra:** 【or】 — ches — tra
- *k* — **psychology:** psy — 【chol】 — o — gy
- *k* — **mechanical:** me — 【chan】 — i — cal
- *f* — **photography:** pho — 【tog】 — ra — phy
- *f* — **catastrophe:** ca — 【tas】 — tro — phy
- *k* — **chrysanthemum:** chry — 【san】 — the — mum
- *f* — **Philadelphia:** Phil — a — 【del】 — phi — a
- *k* — **architectural:** arch — i — 【tec】 — tur — al
- *k* — **choreography:** chor — e — 【og】 — ra — phy
- *k* — **chronological:** chron — o — 【log】 — i — cal
- *k* — **archeology:** arch — e — 【ol】 — o — gy

*A Summary of Accent Patterns is on pages 69 and 70.

/k/ can be spelled five ways.

Use c	• before vowels *a, o,* and *u* • before consonants • at the end of words of two or more syllables	campus clatter shellac
Use k	• before *e, i,* and *y*	kitchen
Use ck	• at the end of a syllable after a short vowel	hockey stocking
Use *que*	• in words of French origin	antique
Use *ch*	• in words of Greek origin	sto*mach*

Write the correct /k/ spelling and copy the word.

C_anary   *canary*
K_ettle   *kettle*
po_ck_et   *pocket*
*techni_que_   *technique*
ch_orus   *chorus*
*_ch_aracter   *character*
traffi_c_   *traffic*

*uni_que_   *unique*
s_ch_olar   *scholar*
*con_que_r   *conquer*
ja_ck_et   *jacket*
*me_ch_anical   *mechanical*
*or_ch_estra   *orchestra*
pictures_que_   *picturesque*

Have another student test you on spelling the starred words. They are practical spelling words.

My score: _____ words correct.

Proofing Practice: Three common List 30 words are misspelled in each of the sentences below. Correct them as shown.

1. Charles went to the ~~farmacy~~ to get some medicine for his ~~aking stomach~~.
   pharmacy · *aching stomach*
2. Her ~~nefew~~ left the ~~charage~~ in a ~~shauffeur~~-driven limousine.
   nephew · *orphanage* · *chauffeur*
3. The ~~Shicago Orkestra~~ played a symphony before the ~~korus~~ sang.
   Chicago Orchestra · *Chorus*
4. Phyllis ~~fotocopied~~ the ~~panflets~~ with the new class ~~schedule~~.
   Photocopied · *pamphlets* · *schedule*
5. Is that ~~monarc~~ butterfly or a ~~moskito~~ that just landed on the ~~orkid~~?
   monarch · *mosquito* · *orchid*

In some words, *ch* as /k/ is preceded by *s. sch* says /sk/.
In some words, *que* as /k/ is preceded by *i. ique* says /ēk/.

The words below have /sk/ and /ēk/ sound patterns. Practice reading them, and see if you can increase your reading speed. Then use the words to complete the puzzle. Refer to a dictionary if necessary.

sch = /sk/		ique = /ēk/	
scheming	scholar	antique	boutique	clique
schedule	scholarship	technique	physique	unique
schooling	schooner	oblique	critique	

Across

4. They crossed the sea on a _____.
6. I love to look at the old furniture in _____ stores.
7. The _____ studied modern philosophy.
9. Do you have a current bus _____?
11. The athlete had a good _____.
12. Good vocal _____ made him a star.
13. He was smart even though his formal _____ ended after seventh grade.

Down

1. She won an athletic _____ to the state university.
2. The actors listened to the director's _____ of the rehearsal.
3. An _____ angle slants to the side.
5. I bought a dress at the new _____.
8. Members of the _____ snubbed the rest of us.
9. The crooks were _____ to rob the bank.
10. You are _____; no one else is like you.

WORKSHEET 30-I

graph is a Greek root that means "writing." Underline *graph* in each word below, and then fill in each blank with the correct word.

autograph   photograph   paragraph   phonograph

graphic   telegraph

1. My teacher told me to write a _paragraph_ about war.
2. Phyllis asked the movie star for his _autograph_.
3. Chris took a _photograph_ of Niagara Falls.
4. David _telegraph_ed urgent news from London.
5. Ralph put the record on the _phonograph_.
6. Drawing, etching, and photography are _graphic_ arts.

graphy is a Greek root that has to do with writing, drawing, study, or science. It is pronounced /grə fē/. Add *graphy* to these word parts, and write each word after its definition. Practice reading the words quickly. Notice that g joins with the previous syllable, which is accented.

ge   o[g]   ra phy

pho   to[g]   ra phy

tel   e[g]   ra phy

cal   li[g]   ra phy

car   to[g]   ra phy

bi   o[g]   ra phy

au to bi   o[g]   ra phy

1. The taking of pictures with a camera — _photography_
2. The written story of a person's life — _biography_
3. The study of the earth's surface, climate, and countries — _geography_
4. Operation or study of the telegraph — _telegraphy_
5. The story of someone's life written by the person — _autobiography_
6. Beautiful handwriting — _calligraphy_
7. The art or work of making maps — _cartography_

10

WORKSHEET 30-J

phon (or *phone*) is a Greek root that means "sound." Underline *phon* or *phone* in the words below, practice reading them, and write each word after the correct definition.

phonics   phonograph   microphone   saxophone   dictaphone

phonetic   telephone   megaphone   symphony

1. An instrument that records and reproduces sound, such as a stereo — _phonograph_
2. A device that transmits conversations a long distance — _telephone_
3. A device that records sounds or makes sounds louder — _microphone_
4. The science of speech sounds — _phonics_
5. A large horn used by cheerleaders to make their voices louder — _megaphone_
6. Spelled by phonic rules — _phonetic_
7. A machine for recording the messages that someone dictates into it — _dictaphone_
8. A musical instrument — _saxophone_
9. Music played by an orchestra — _symphony_

phil is a Greek root that means "love." Underline *phil* in the words below, and write each word in the correct blank.

philanthropist   Phillip   philosophy   philosopher   Philadelphia

philodendron   philanthropy

Phillip was a deep-thinking scholar, a _philosopher_. He lived in _Philadelphia_, the City of Brotherly Love. One day a lovely green _philodendron_ was delivered to his office. Attached was a note from a generous _philanthropist_. His _philanthropy_ awarded Phillip one thousand dollars for him to continue his studies in _philosophy_.

Cacophony: Guess what this word means. Then look it up for extra credit. _harsh sound_

11

WORKSHEET 30–L

Read the following sentences and circle all the List 30 words that you can find.

1. The (psychiatrist's) (charisma) created eager audiences for his lectures on (melancholy).
2. (Phoebe) got a (unique) remedy for her (stomachache) at the (pharmacy).
3. (Christine) had to choose an (orchid), a (philodendron), or a (chrysanthemum) for her friend's (boutique).
4. The (mosquito) is not a carrier of (cholera) or (typhoid) fever.
5. (Phyllis) was a first-rate (scholar) in (chemistry), (architecture), and (psychology).
6. My nephew (Christopher) is a (mechanic) on a (schooner) in the (Philippines).
7. Your (physician) may caution you about (chronic) (physical) problems caused by (liquor).
8. The (chauffeur) drove a (chemist) and an (architect) from (Philadelphia) to (Chicago).
9. The (monarch) invited the (orphans) to play (charades) at his (chateau).
10. (Charlotte) and (Charles) can't (decipher) the message on this (brochure).

Look at List 30. Choose five words and write them in sentences below.

Sentences – Teacher corrected.

_____

_____

_____

_____

_____

Take out a piece of blank paper. Your teacher will dictate three of the sentences above for you to write.

You have completed the worksheets for List 30. Now it is time to check your accuracy in reading and spelling. Read and spell ten words selected by your teacher, and record your scores on the Accuracy Checklist. Work toward 90–100 percent accuracy.

When you have achieved 90–100 percent accuracy in reading, build up your reading speed. Decide on your rate goal with your teacher. Record your rate on the Proficiency Graph.

My goal for reading List 30 is _____ words per minute with two or fewer errors.

13

WORKSHEET 30–K

psych is a Greek root that means "mind." Add *psych* to the word parts below, practice reading the words, and write each word in the correct blank.

psychology
psychic
psychoanalysis
psychiatrist
psychologist

A psychiatrist has an M.D. degree and treats people who have problems that are troubling them. A psychologist studies the mind and behavior but does not have an M.D. degree. His or her field of study is called psychology. Sigmund Freud developed the process of psychoanalysis. A psychic claims to see into the future and past.

photo is a Greek root that means "light." Underline *photo* in the words below, practice reading them, and write each word in the correct blank.

photography   photoelectric   photograph   photogenic   photocopy

photographer   telephoto

1. The photographer won the photography contest with a telephoto lens.
2. A photoelectric cell is like an electric eye and may be used to open doors automatically.
3. If you are photogenic, you look good in pictures.
4. Please photocopy this report for me; we need a copy for the files.

chron is a Greek root that means "time." Underline *chron* in the words below and practice reading them.

chronic—lasting a long time

chronological—arranged in the time order in which events happened

synchronize—agree in time; occur at the same time

Bonus: Guess what these three words mean. Then look up their definitions for extra credit.

chronologist — an expert in measuring time

chronometer — a device for measuring time

chronology — the science of measuring time

12

When c is followed by e, i, or y, it has its soft sound, /s/, as in face, city, and cycle. Followed by any other letter, it has its hard sound, /k/, as in cat, crop, cute, and coat.

In the following words, identify, trace in red, and then copy all the combinations of ci, ce, and cy. Say the sounds aloud as you trace the letters. e and i often have a short-vowel or schwa sound; y says /ē/ at the end of a word.

ci = /sī/		ce = /sē/		cy = /sē/	
census	ce	centipede	ce	faucet	ce
citizen	ci	rancid	ci	Cincinnati	ci
celestial	ce	anticipate	ci	reciprocate	ci
stencil	ci	recipe	ci	icicle	ci
emergency	cy	successful	ce	accentuate	ce
accidental	ci	infancy	cy	democracy	cy
irascible	ci	incinerator	ci	ulcer	ce
vaccinate	ci	succinct	ci	vacancy	cy
necessary	ce	concentration	ce	accessible	ce

When does c have its soft sound, /s/?

c has its soft sound, /s/, when it is followed by e, i, or y.

Pronounce the following syllables in which c says /s/. Then have your teacher or a classmate time you to see how long it takes you to read the list. See if you can improve your time with practice.

cen	cir	cel	cit	cess
cer	cent	cid	cept	cend
cym	cin	cil	cip	cem

Review: When c is followed by e, i, or y, it has its soft sound, /s/. Followed by any other letter, it has its hard sound, /k/.

Review: When c is followed by e, i, or y, it has its soft sound, /s/. Followed by any other letter, it has its hard sound, /k/.

Sometimes soft c is followed by a long vowel. Read and time yourself on these syllables.

ceed	cize	cite	ceal	ci
cise	cide	ceil	cere	cy*

Circle only those syllables in which c says /s/. Then write the syllables with soft c, saying them aloud as you write.

(cir)	cir	(cel)	cel	cad		excellent	exce(llent)
(cim)	cim	(cite)	cite	clem		reception	re(cep)tion
(cere)	cere	crad		cym	(cym)	recite	re(cite)
(ceal)	ceal	(cess)	cess	cin	(cin)	cinnamon	(cin)namon
cor		(ceed)	ceed	cer	(cer)	concern	con(cern)
crin		cal		cept	(cept)	criticize	criti(cize)

receptive	re(cep)tive
excessive	exce(ss)ive
December	De(cem)ber
cymbal	(cym)bal
orchestra	orchestra
ceiling	(ceil)ing

Circle the syllables with soft c in the words below.

re(ced)ing	exer(cise)	physical
corduroy	sin(cer)ity	bi(cyc)le
(cer)tificate	conclusion	cir(cu)lar
con(cea)led	suc(ceed)	(Cid)er
(cir)cus	ex(cept)	pen(cil)
(cel)ebrate	de(cide)	re(cent)

*cy says both /sē/ and /sī/.

WORKSHEET 31-C

Your teacher will dictate some syllables for you to spell. Say the syllable aloud as you write it. Use c for the /s/ sound.

1. cip   4. cel   6. cen   8. cess
2. cite   5. cin   7. ceed   9. cit
3. cept   10. cide

Write two ways to spell the syllable /sər/ in soft-c, multisyllabic words.

cir   cer

Write two ways to spell the syllable /si/ in soft-c, multisyllabic words.

ci   cy

When do you use c to spell /s/ in multisyllabic words?

Use c to spell /s/ in multisyllabic words when it is followed by e, i, or y.

Your teacher will dictate some words. Write the first syllable in the words you hear.

1. ci   3. cem   5. cel   7. cir
2. cig   4. ce   6. cit   8. civ

Use the letters on the right to make multisyllabic words out of cent.

cent**er** → center	con**cent**rate
cent**ury** → century	**cent**imeter
accent → accent	**ac**cent**uate**
cent**ral** → central	**cent**ipede
recent → recent	

ac
re
ury
imeter
ac — uate
er
ipede
con — rate
ral

17

Pronounce and combine the syllables. Then cover the divided word and practice reading the whole word. Underline the soft c in the whole word.

va can cy	vacancy	prev a lence	prevalence
suc cinct	succinct	cel e brate	celebrate
cir cum stance	circumstance	cin na mon	cinnamon
i ci cle	icicle	e mer gen cy	emergency
cer ti fi cate	certificate	in cin er ate	incinerate
ac cen tu ate	accentuate	an ti ci pate	anticipate
cen ti pede	centipede	con cen tra tion	concentration
in ci dent	incident	ac cel er a tor	accelerator
ex cel lent	excellent	tā ci turn	taciturn
gro cer y	grocery	prin ci pal	principal

Underline the soft c's. Then match the syllables to make real words. Say each word aloud as you write it.

pen ⟍ cel → cancel
can ⟋ cil → pencil
cir ⟍ cense → license
li ⟋ cus → circus

spi ⟍ cent → recent
re ⟋ cer → cancer
can ⟍ cle → circle
cir ⟋ cy → spicy

Unscramble these multisyllabic words.

ci de sive → decisive
e ci ty so → society
in cyl der → cylinder
cin Cin ti na → Cincinnati
nate ci vac → vaccinate

18

WORKSHEET 31-E

Your teacher will dictate some words. Sound out each word as you write the missing syllable(s). Then write the whole word, saying it aloud as you spell it.

		Copy	ABC Order
*1.	cen ter	center	accelerator
*2.	can cel	cancel	cancel
*3.	cir cle	circle	celebrate
4.	in fan cy	infancy	census
5.	cen sus	census	center
6.	ul cer	ulcer	certificate
*7.	con cern	concern	Cincinnati
*8.	suc cess ful	successful	circle
*9.	ex cept	except	concern
*10.	gro cer y	grocery	deficit
11.	ac cel er a tor	accelerator	except
12.	Cin cin na ti	Cincinnati	fascinate
*13.	fas ci nate	fascinate	grocery
14.	def i cit	deficit	infancy
*15.	cel e brate	celebrate	successful
*16.	cer ti fi cate	certificate	ulcer

Now go back and write the words in alphabetical order.

Have another student test you on spelling the starred words. They are practical spelling words.

My score: _____ words correct.

WORKSHEET 31-F

cir is always found at the beginning of words. Fill in the missing syllable, cir, and write each word next to its definition.

			Definition	Answer
*	cir	cle	1. Event; fact	circumstance
	cir	cuit	2. Having a shape like a circle	circular
*	cir	cus	3. A round figure	circle
*	cir	cum stance	4. To pass from person to person	circulate
*	cir	cu lar	5. Careful; cautious	circumspect
	cir	cu late	6. Electric current flows over it	circuit
	cir	cum spect	7. A traveling show	circus

Sometimes cer is found at the beginning of a word.

				Answer
*	cer	tain		certain
*	cer	ti fi cate		certificate
	cer	ti fied		certified

However, cer is usually found in the middle or at the end of words. Fill in the missing letters, cer, and write each word next to its definition.

			Definition	Answer
*can	cer		8. A type of store	grocery
ul	cer		9. Interest in something	concern
*con	cer	n	10. A disease; a harmful growth	cancer
con	cer	t	11. An open sore	ulcer
*gro	cer	y	12. A musical performance	concert

Have another student test you on spelling the starred words. They are practical spelling words.

My score: _____ words correct.

Review: cir and cer spell /sər/ at the beginning of a word.

Fill in the missing syllable, *ci*, in the words below. *ci* says /sĭ/. Then fill in each blank with the correct word. Use a dictionary to look up unfamiliar words.

*vac _ci_ nate	1. A large town	city
*prin _ci_ pal	2. A happening; an event	incident
*i _ci_ cle	3. Directions for preparing food	recipe
*ac _ci_ dent	4. Give a shot to prevent disease	vaccinate
ta _ci_ turn	5. Head of a school	principal
* _ci_ ty	6. Unlucky happening	accident
anti _ci_ pate	7. A member of a nation	citizen
* _ci_ tizen	8. Hanging piece of ice	icicle
*re _ci_ pe	9. Look forward to	anticipate
* _ci_ vilized	10. Not fond of talking	taciturn
*in _ci_ dent	11. Having a highly developed culture	civilized

In the following words, the missing syllable, *ci*, says /sĭ/ and is accented. Practice writing these words; then use them in a sentence.

de _ci_ sive _____decisive_____   *so _ci_ ety _____society_____

_____Answers will vary._____

Have another student test you on spelling the starred words. They are practical spelling words.

My score: _____ words correct.

Review: At the beginning of words, /sər/ is spelled _cir_ or _cer_.

In the middle or at the end of words, /sər/ is spelled _cer_.

Since *y* has three vowel sounds, *cy* also has three sounds.

cy says /sē/ as in *fancy*.
cy says /sī/ as in *cyclone*.
cy says /sĭ/ as in *cymbal*.

cy says /sē/ at the end of a word. Fill in each blank with *cy*, copy the words, and write them in alphabetical order.

	Copy	ABC Order
vacan _cy_	vacancy	accuracy
emergen _cy_	emergency	democracy
democra _cy_	democracy	emergency
spi _cy_	spicy	spicy
accura _cy_	accuracy	vacancy

cy says /sī/ when it is an open syllable at the beginning or in the middle of a word. Fill in each blank with *cy*, copy the words, and write them in alphabetical order.

_cy_ clone	cyclone	cyanide
en _cy_ clopedia	encyclopedia	cycle
_cy_ anide	cyanide	cyclist
_cy_ clist	cyclist	cyclone
_cy_ press	cypress	cypress
_cy_ cle	cycle	encyclopedia

cy says /sĭ/ when it is part of a closed syllable and in some other words. Fill in each blank with *cy*, copy the words, and write them in alphabetical order.

_cy_ linder	cylinder	bicycle
_cy_ gnet	cygnet	cygnet
_cy_ mbal	cymbal	cylinder
bi _cy_ cle	bicycle	cymbal
tri _cy_ cle	tricycle	cynic
_cy_ nic	cynic	tricycle

Use the words from Worksheet 31–H to complete the puzzle.

Across

*3. A form of government
5. A type of evergreen tree
6. A percussion instrument
7. A young swan
8. One who believes that the motives of others are selfish and insincere
11. A violent windstorm
*14. A reference book
15. A three wheeler
*16. A two wheeler

Down

1. Well-seasoned, as food
*2. A crisis; a situation needing immediate action
4. To occur over and over; a root meaning "wheel"
5. A hollow body shaped like a roller
9. A bicycle rider
*10. Correctness; exactness
13. A powerful poison

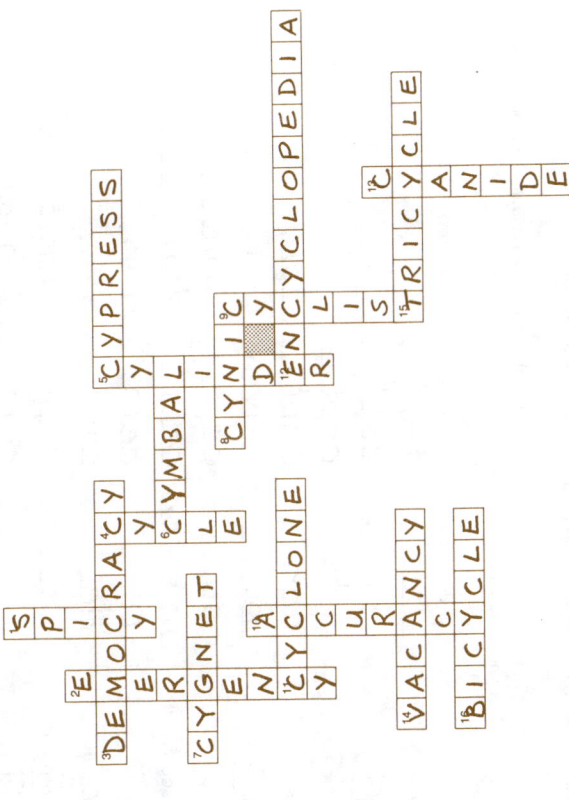

Have another student test you on spelling the starred words. They are practical spelling words.

My score: _____ words correct.

23

Many English words come from the Latin root *cedere*. In English words this root is spelled *cess*, *ceed*, and *cede*. The meaning of *cedere* is "to go." We can add a prefix such as *re*, which means "back," to the root. The word *recede* literally means "to go back."

Circle the root in each of the following words, and then write the separate word parts, saying the words aloud as you write them.

	Prefix	Root			Prefix	Root
suc(cess)	suc	cess		suc(ceed)	suc	ceed
re(cess)	re	cess		re(cede)	re	cede
ex(cess)	ex	cess		ex(ceed)	ex	ceed
pro(cess)	pro	cess		pro(ceed)	pro	ceed
con(cede)	con	cede		pre(cede)	pre	cede

	Prefix	Root	Suffix(es) or Ending(s)
suc(cess)or	suc	cess	or
suc(ceed)ed	suc	ceed	ed
con(cess)ion	con	cess	ion
pro(ceed)ing	pro	ceed	ing
re(cess)ion	re	cess	ion
pro(cede)ure*	pro	ced	ure
inter(cede)ed*	inter	ced	ed
suc(cess)fully	suc	cess	fully
pre(cede)nce*	pre	ced	ence
ne(cess)ity	ne	cess	ity
ex(ceed)ingly	ex	ceed	ingly
pro(cess)ional	pro	cess	ional

*The final *e* is dropped from the root when an ending that begins with a vowel is added.

24

WORKSHEET 31-K

Many English words come from the Latin root *capere*. In English words this root is spelled *cept*, *cep*, and *ceive*. The meaning of *capere* is "to take." We can add a prefix such as *ex*, which means "out," to the root. The word *except* literally means "to take out."

Circle the root in each of the following words, and then write the separate word parts, saying the words aloud as you write them.

	Prefix(es)	Root	Suffix(es) or Ending(s)
ac(cept)	ac	cept	
ex(cept)	ex	cept	
inter(cept)	inter	cept	
con(cep)tion	con	cept	ion
re(ceive)	re	ceive	
sus(cept)ible	sus	cept	ible
mis(con)(cep)tion	mis con	cept	ion
re(cep)tion	re	cept	ion
de(cep)tive	de	cept	ive
ac(cept)ance	ac	cept	ance
ex(cept)ional	ex	cept	ion al
inter(cept)ed	inter	cept	ed
re(cep)tionist	re	cept	ion ist
ac(cept)able	ac	cept	able
de(ceive)	de	ceive	
pre(con)(cep)tion	pre con	cept	ion

The spelling of the root in *receipt* is different from those above. What is the silent letter in *receipt?* __p__ How many letters are in this word? __7__ Practice it.

re C e ipt   r e ce i p t   r e c e i p t   receipt

25

WORKSHEET 31-L

Certain spelling patterns recur in soft-c words. Recognizing these patterns makes spelling them easier. Fill in the blanks with the common pattern and write the words.

Add *cen*		Copy		Add *cel*		Copy
re	cen t	recent	can	cel	cancel	
	cen ter	center		cel ebrate	celebrate	
des	cen d	descend		cel ery	celery	
ac	cen t	accent	ac	cel erate	accelerate	
	cen sus	census	de	cel erate	decelerate	
li	cen se	license				
	cen tury	century				
	cen tral	central				
	cen tipede	centipede				
con	cen tration	concentration				

Add *cin*		Copy
fas	cin ate	fascinate
vac	cin ate	vaccinate
in	cin erate	incinerate
	cin namon	cinnamon
	cin der	cinder

Add *cil*		Copy
pen	cil	pencil
sten	cil	stencil
fa	cil itate	facilitate
fa	cil ity	facility

cide is a root that comes from the Latin word meaning "to kill." Add the root *cide* to the word parts below. Then write each word after its definition. Use a dictionary to look up unfamiliar words.

herbi	cide	1. The act of killing oneself on purpose	suicide
homi	cide		herbicide
sui	cide	2. A chemical used to kill weeds	
insecti	cide	3. A chemical used to kill insects	insecticide
		4. Manslaughter; murder	homicide

26

Your teacher will dictate some practical spelling words that contain the soft *c* sound. Say the words aloud as you write them under the correct heading.

cept	cir	cer
accept	circus	concert
except	circle	certain

cess	cen	cel
success	center	celebrate
recess	century	excellent
	license	
	concentrate	

ci		cise
society		exercise

cy	ci	cere
vacancy	recipe	cereal
emergency	accident	sincere
	citizen	

ceive		cide
receive		decide

Proofing Practice: Two common List 31 words are misspelled in each of the sentences below. Correct them as shown.

               receipt   bicycle

1. Are you certain you got a ~~receet~~ when you purchased your ~~bicicle~~?
                  Cereal   grocery
2. Francis will buy celery, peanut butter, and ~~serial~~ at the ~~grosery~~ store.
          Concentrate   exercises
3. Mr. Percy can ~~concintrate~~ on his studies much better after he ~~exercizes~~.
                 license   accident
4. Lucille lost her driver's ~~lisense~~ after her automobile ~~acsident~~ last December.

Review the accent patterns below. Write the words by syllables, putting the accented syllables in the boxes.

The accent is usually on the first syllable in two-syllable words.

census | cen | sus   circuit | cir | cuit

fancy | fan | cy   pencil | pen | cil

Two-syllable words that have a prefix in the first syllable and a root in the second syllable are usually accented on the second syllable.

concern   con | cern | receive   re | ceive |

recite   re | cite | decide   de | cide |

The accent is usually on the first syllable in three-syllable words.

ancestor | an | ces tor   vaccinate | vac | ci nate

citizen | cit | i zen   circumstance | cir | cum stance

The accent is usually on the second syllable in three-syllable words that contain a prefix, root, and suffix.

deceitful   de | ceit | ful   decisive   de | ci | sive

recital   re | ci | tal   recession   re | ces | sion

The accent is usually on the second syllable in four-syllable words.

anticipate   an | ti | ci pate

necessity   ne | ces | si ty

WORKSHEET 31-O

Write the word from below that can be used in place of the italicized word(s). Then complete the puzzle. Use a dictionary to look up the meaning of unfamiliar words.

century taciturn recipe vaccination census

succinct concentrate vacancy proceed cancel

center descend

1. The U.S. government took a *count of the people* in 1980. (8 Across)   census
2. I cannot *think clearly* when there is so much noise! (10 Across)   concentrate
3. Use the elevator to *go down* to the lower level. (1 Down)   descend
4. I want to *stop* my subscription to the magazine. (7 Down)   cancel
5. The next *100 years* will bring many scientific advances. (11 Across)   century
6. Do not *go ahead* until I tell you to do so. (2 Across)   proceed
7. Have you had your *"shot"* for smallpox yet? (3 Across)   vaccination
8. John is a *quiet* person. He hardly ever talks. (9 Across)   taciturn
9. The council is planning a park for the *middle* of the city. (4 Down)   center
10. Do you have the *directions* for making fudge? (5 Down)   recipe
11. There is no *empty space* at this motel. The rooms are all filled. (3 Down)   vacancy
12. The president gave a *clear and concise* speech last night. (6 Across)   succinct

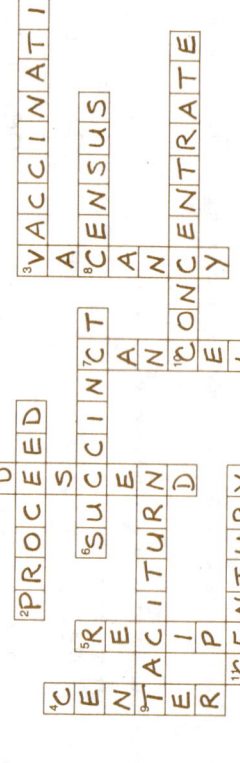

29

WORKSHEET 31-P

The words *accept* and *except* are often confused because they sound alike. It will be easier to tell them apart if you understand the meaning of the prefix in each word.

 Accept means "to take *toward* oneself; to receive."
 Except means "to take *out* of; to exclude."

Fill in each blank with *accept* or *except*.

1. Everyone in the Philosophy Society went to the movie __except__ Margaret Prentice, who was sick.
2. The mail carrier asked me to __accept__ a package for the neighbors.
3. My Aunt Alice will not __accept__ money from anyone.
4. Maurice has been in every state __except__ Alaska and Hawaii.
5. Mr. Quincy wants to __accept__ the job he was offered yesterday.
6. Some people will simply not __accept__ people who are different.
7. Everyone __except__ me wanted to go to the French restaurant near the university.
8. I do not know anyone __except__ Bruce who is tall enough to play center.
9. All the girls in the family __except__ Candace are good singers.
10. Please __accept__ my condolences for your misfortune.

Write one sentence that contains both the words *except* and *accept*.

__Answers will vary.__

Proofing Practice: Two common List 31 words are misspelled in each of the sentences below. Correct them as shown.

1. Stacy is quite ~~certin~~ *certain* she will go to the rock ~~conert~~ *concert*.
2. Nothing ~~suhceeds~~ *succeeds* like ~~sukcess~~ *success*.
3. It is ~~neccessary~~ *necessary* to keep the ~~emergeney~~ *emergency* exit closed at all times.

30

Read the following sentences and circle all the List 31 words that you can find.

1. Bernice's (recent) (success) was due to her (excellent) work.
2. The (homicide) detective had (access) to the (scene) of the (accident)
3. The (bicycle) rider is (sincere) in his belief that (exercise) is (necessary) for good health.
4. The (fancy) foods can be found in the (center) aisle of the (grocery) store.
5. (Cynthia) was (certain) that the (icicles) on the roof would cause the (ceiling) to leak.
6. (Felice) (decided) to (accept) the (criticism) without comment, hoping that it would soon (cease).
7. The gift (certificate) stated that (Priscilla) (Dorrance) was entitled to (cereal,) apple (cider,) and a (citrus) fruit of her (choice).
8. Draw a (circle) in the (center) of the paper with your red (pencil).
9. During the (emergency) the victims (received) help in an (emergency) room set up in the Civic (center).
10. Smoking (cigars) and (cigarettes) may cause lung (cancer).

Look at List 31. Choose five words and write them in sentences below.

Sentences — Teacher corrected.
_____
_____
_____

Take out a piece of blank paper. Your teacher will dictate three of the sentences above for you to write.

You have completed the worksheets for List 31. Now it is time to check your accuracy in reading and spelling. Read and spell ten words selected by your teacher, and record your scores on the Accuracy Checklist. Work toward 90–100 percent accuracy.
When you have achieved 90–100 percent accuracy in reading, build up your reading speed. Decide on your rate goal with your teacher. Record your rate on the Proficiency Graph.

My goal for reading List 31 is _____ words per minute with two or fewer errors.

Fill in each blank with a word from below that makes sense in the sentence.

cyclone	Society	faucet	Cancer	accelerate
accents	receive	principal	citizens	anticipates
cinnamon	license	rancid	necessary	grocery

1. Cindy Lawrence had to retake her driver's test in order to renew her license.
2. When you go to the grocery store, please buy me a box of cinnamon.
3. Can Clarence fix the dripping faucet?
4. You must accelerate quickly when you drive onto the freeway.
5. The senior citizens in our town volunteer at the election booths.
6. I wouldn't eat the leftover fish—it is rancid.
7. It is necessary that you come to the school board meeting. The principal wants to discuss some important issues.
8. The cyclone damaged many homes last summer.
9. Cecelia anticipates a good response from the mailings. She hopes to receive several donations from members of the American Cancer Society.
10. You can tell that Cedric and Percy are from England. They have British accents.

Unscramble the words below and spell them correctly in the blanks and circles. All the words can be found in the list above.

NOCYCLE   CYCLONE
SAYSCREEN   NECESSARY
DINCAR   RANCID

Unscramble the letters you have written in the circles to make another word from the list above:
LICENSE

When *g* is followed by *e*, *i*, or *y*, it usually has its soft sound, /j/, as in *cage*, *giant*, and *gym*. Followed by any other letter, it has its hard sound, /g/, as in *goat*, *grin*, and *gas*.

In the following words, identify, trace in red, and then copy all the combinations of *ge*, *gi*, and *gy*. Say the sounds aloud as you trace the letters. *e* and *i* often have a short-vowel or schwa sound; *y* says /ē/ at the end of a word.

ge = /jē/		*gi* = /jī/		*gy* = /jē/	
gentle	*ge*	tragedy	*ge*	suggest	*ge*
longitude	*gi*	energy	*gy*	margin	*gi*
original	*gi*	generate	*ge*	urgency	*ge*
longevity	*ge*	gesture	*ge*	eligible	*gi*
register	*gi*	gelatin	*ge*	fugitive	*gi*
clergy	*gy*	vigil	*gi*	energetic	*ge*
logic	*gi*	legend	*ge*	genuine	*ge*
regiment	*gi*	allergy	*gy*	digestion	*ge*
ingenuity	*ge*	stingy	*gy*	emergency	*ge*

When does *g* have its soft sound, /j/?

g usually has its soft sound, /j/, when it is followed by e, i, or y.

Pronounce the following syllables in which *g* says /j/. Then have your teacher or a classmate time you to see how long it takes you to read the list. See if you can improve your time with practice.

gen	gic	gest	ge	gyp
germ	gel	gem	gin	gil
gi	ger	gev	gir	gy*

Review: *g* usually says /jē/ and /jī/.

*gy says both /jē/ and /jī/.

Review: When *g* is followed by *e*, *i*, or *y*, it usually has its soft sound, /j/. Followed by any other letter, it has its hard sound, /g/.

Circle only those syllables in which *g* says /j/. Then write the syllables with soft *g*, saying them aloud as you write.

(gin)	*gin*	gran	———	(gy)	*gy*
(germ)	*germ*	gon	———	(ge)	*ge*
glib	———	grad	———	(gel)	*gel*
(gyp)	*gyp*	gum	———	(gir)	*gir*
(gil)	*gil*	(gic)	*gic*	gab	———
(gest)	*gest*	(ger)	*ger*	(gi)	*gi*
gal	———	(gen)	*gen*	(gev)	*gev*

Circle the syllables with soft *g* in the words below.

emer(ge)ncy	(ger)micide	aller(gic)	an(gel)	E(gy)pt	grocery
(ge)ometry	ori(gin)	(gen)eralization	(gel)atin	di(ge)stion	eli(gi)ble
messen(ger)	(gi)raffe	vi(gil)		lon(ge)vity	sug(ge)st
dan(ger)ous	paragraph	(gen)erous	indul(ge)nt	magnify	mar(gin)
(gi)gantic	(gen)eration	tra(gic)		ener(gy)	re(gis)ter
degree	(ge)nius	(gy)mnastics			
(gen)tle	le(gis)late	(gi)ant	col(le)ge		

Your teacher will dictate some syllables for you to spell. Say the syllable aloud as you write it. Use g for the /j/ sound.

1. gen   3. gel   5. gic   7. gest
2. ger   4. gi   6. gin   8. gem

Write two ways to spell the syllable /jē/ in soft-g, multisyllabic words.

ge   gy

How do you spell /j/ at the end of a word? (Clue: At the zoo, tigers are kept in a ca ge___.)

ge

What three letters do these words have in common?

Gypsy   Egypt   gypsum   gyp

How do you spell the /jĭp/ sound?   gyp

When do you use g to spell /j/ in multisyllabic words?

You usually use g to spell /j/ in multisyllabic words when it is followed by e, i, or y.

Your teacher will dictate some words. Write the first syllable in the words you hear.

1. ge om e try   6. gel a tin
2. gem stone   7. gin ger
3. ges ture   8. Gyp sy
4. gen tle
5. ger mi cide

Pronounce and combine the syllables. Then cover the divided word and practice reading the whole word. Underline the soft g in the whole word.

gen u ine	genuine	in dul gent	indulgent	
tan gi ble	tangible	sug ges tion	suggestion	
gen er ous	generous	mes sen ger	messenger	
im ag ine	imagine	leg is late	legislate	
trag e dy	tragedy	lon gi tude	longitude	
al ler gy	allergy	a strin gent	astringent	
fu gi tive	fugitive	ex ag ger ate	exaggerate	*
gen er al	general	e mer gen cy	emergency	
leg i ble	legible	en er get ic	energetic	
reg is ter	register	lon gev i ty	longevity	
gen tle man	gentleman	con tin gen cy	contingency	

Underline the soft g's. Then match the syllables to make real words. Say each word aloud as you write it.

gen — ant → giant
gi — lege → college
col — gine → engine
en — tle → gentle

a — gest → digest
di — gent → agent
sur — end → legend
leg — geon → surgeon

Unscramble these multisyllabic words.

tion ges di — digestion
ol ge gy o — geology
ment en gage — engagement
phy og ra ge — geography
nas gym tics — gymnastics
e om ge try — geometry

* Students may underline either g or gg.

WORKSHEET 32-E

Your teacher will dictate some words. Sound out each word as you write the missing syllable(s). Then write the whole word, saying it aloud as you spell it.

	Copy	ABC Order
*1. __gen__ tle	gentle	allergy
2. Gyp __sy__	Gypsy	dangerous
3. __al__ ler __gy__	allergy	gelatin
*4. sug __ges__ tion	suggestion	gentle
*5. __pas__ sen __ger__	Passenger	genuine
6. __log__ ic	logic	giant
7. ur __gent__	urgent	gigantic
*8. mar __gin__	margin	Gypsy
*9. __gi__ gan __tic__	gigantic	legislate
10. __sub__ merge	submerge	logic
11. __gel__ a tin	gelatin	margin
*12. __leg__ is __late__	legislate	passenger
*13. dan __ger__ __ous__	dangerous	submerge
*14. __gi__ ant	giant	suggestion
15. __gen__ u ine	genuine	tragedy
*16. __trag__ e dy	tragedy	urgent

Now go back and write the words in alphabetical order.

Have another student test you on spelling the starred words. They are practical spelling words.

My score: _____ words correct.

Fill in the missing letters, *gi*, in the words below. *gi* says /jĭ/ or /jə/. Then write each word next to its definition. Use a dictionary to look up unfamiliar words.

lon __gi__ tude	1. Capable of being touched	tangible
le __gi__ ble	2. A person who is fleeing	fugitive
eli __gi__ ble	3. Sign up on a list	register
re __gi__ ment	4. Easy to read; clear	legible
fu __gi__ tive	5. Make laws	legislate
*re __gi__ ster	6. Unit of an army	regiment
tan __gi__ ble	7. Properly qualified	eligible
*le __gi__ slate	8. Distance east or west of the meridian	longitude

In the following words, the missing syllable, *gi*, says /jī/. Practice writing these words.

*__gi__ ant   giant   *__gi__ gantic   gigantic

Have another student test you on spelling the starred words. They are practical spelling words.

My score: _____ words correct.

Find and circle the ten words above in the puzzle below. The words can be found in a straight line across or up and down. Write the leftover letters in the blanks below.

```
L O N G I T U D E R E G I M E N T
L E G I S L A T E F E I O R Y C O M
G I G A N T I C E S E L I G I B L E
A F T N E R G F U G I T I V E G H A
S I T A N G I B L E S S O F T S O
U R E G I S T E R N L E G I B L E D
```

I F E, L, OR Y COMES AFTER G,
G HAS ITS SOFT SOUND.

WORKSHEET 32-G

Since *y* has three vowel sounds, *gy* also has three sounds.

gy says /jē/ as in sting*y*.
gy says /jī/ as in *gy*rate.
gy says /jǐ/ as in *gy*m.

gy says /jē/ at the end of a word. Fill in each blank with *gy*, and write the whole word.

	Copy	ABC Order
en er gy	energy	allergy
al ler gy	allergy	clergy
cler gy	clergy	dingy
stin gy	stingy	energy
din gy	dingy	geology
ge ol o gy	geology	psychology
psy chol o gy	psychology	stingy

gy says /jī/ in a closed syllable. Fill in each blank with *gy*, and write the whole word.

	Copy	ABC Order
gy p sy	gypsy	Egypt
gy m nas tics	gymnastics	gymnastics
E gy pt	Egypt	gypsum
gy p sum	gypsum	gypsy

gy says /jī/ only rarely. Practice these words.

gy rate gyrate   gy ro scope gyroscope

gi says /jī/ in an open syllable.

gi ant giant   gi gan tic gigantic

WORKSHEET 32-H

Some common English words come from the Latin root *gerere*. In English words this root is spelled *gest* or *ges*. The meaning of *gerere* is "to bear or carry." Thus, the word *gestation* refers to child bearing, or pregnancy.

Circle the root in each of the following words, and then write the separate word parts, saying the words aloud as you write them.

	Prefix(es)	Root	Suffix
suggested	sug	gest	ed
digesting	di	gest	ing
gesture		gest	ure
suggestion	sug	gest	ion
digestion	di	gest	ion
indigestion	in di	gest	ion
suggested	sug	gest	ed
digestive	di	gest	ive
gesticulate		gest	iculate

Fill in the blanks with words from above.

1. Gerald _suggested_ that we go on a picnic. What a wonderful _suggestion_!
2. George suffers from _indigestion_. There is something wrong with his _digestive_ tract.
3. Georgina often makes _gestures_ with her hands when she talks. She _gesticulates_.
4. You will have better _digestion_ if you chew your food well.

On a separate sheet of paper, practice spelling these common words that end in *geon* and *gion*.

region   religion   surgeon   pigeon

WORKSHEET 32-J

Review the accent patterns below. Write the words by syllables, putting the accented syllables in the boxes.

The accent is usually on the first syllable in two-syllable words.

gentle   [gen] tle

college   [col] lege

giant   [gi] ant

dingy   [din] gy

Two-syllable words that have a prefix in the first syllable and a root in the second syllable are usually accented on the second syllable.

enrage   en [rage]

submerge   sub [merge]

infringe   in [fringe]

engage   en [gage]

The accent is usually on the first syllable in three-syllable words.

gelatin   [gel] a tin

allergy   [al] ler gy

germicide   [ger] mi cide

regiment   [reg] i ment

The accent is usually on the second syllable in three-syllable words that contain a prefix, root, and suffix.

indulgent   in [dul] gent

engagement   en [gage] ment

digestion   di [ges] tion

religion   re [li] gion

The accent is usually on the second syllable in four-syllable words.

gesticulate   ges [tic] u late

contingency   con [tin] gen cy

WORKSHEET 32-I

Certain spelling patterns recur in soft-g words. Recognizing these patterns makes spelling them easier. Fill in the blanks with the common patterns and write the words.

Add *gen*

	Copy
gen tle	gentle
emer gen cy	emergency
gen eral	general
a gen t	agent
gen erous	generous
le gen d	legend
gen uine	genuine
ur gen cy	urgency

Add *gin*

	Copy
gin ger	ginger
mar gin	margin
ori gin al	original
ima gin e	imagine
en gin e	engine

Add *ge*

	Copy
indul ge	indulge
colle ge	college
enga ge	engage
submer ge	submerge
enra ge	enrage
infrin ge	infringe
mer ge	merge
wa ge	wage
pa ge	page

Add *ger*

	Copy
gin ger	ginger
wa ger	wager
messen ger	messenger
passen ger	passenger
exag ger ate	exaggerate
Ger man	German
ger micide	germicide
dan ger ous	dangerous

Review: When does g have its soft sound, /j/? Write the rule.

g usually has its soft sound, /j/, when it is followed by e, i, or y.

gy says /jē/ at the end of a word. gy says /jī/ or /jĭ/ in the middle or at the beginning of a word.

Complete the puzzle with the gy and gi words below.

*energy	*Egypt	dingy	stingy	gyroscope
Gypsy	allergy	gyrate	gypsum	*gymnastics
clergy	*giant		*gigantic	gymnasium

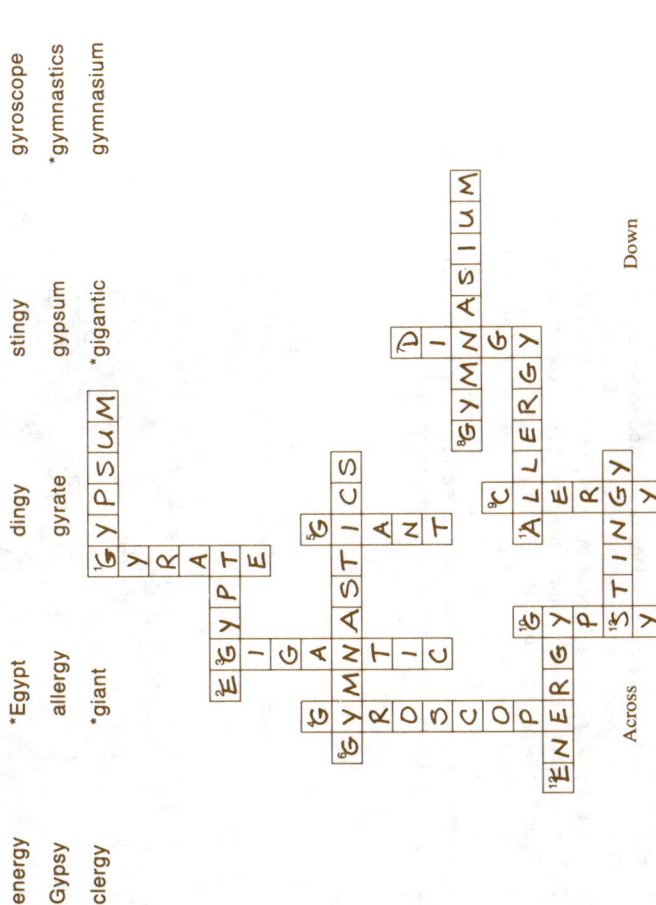

Across
1. A mineral
2. A country in Africa
6. Physical exercises
8. The room where gym class is held
11. Hay fever
12. Power; vigor
13. Opposite of generous

Down
1. Move in a circle; rotate
3. Huge
4. A wheel in a ring used to measure a ship's stability
5. A huge creature found in folk tales
7. Dirty looking
9. Ministers
10. Person from a wandering tribe

Have another student test you on spelling the starred words. They are practical spelling words.

My score: _____ words correct.

Your teacher will dictate some practical spelling words that contain the soft-g sound. Say the words aloud as you write them under the correct heading.

gen	ger	gī
gentle	German	giant
general	dangerous	gigantic
generous	passenger	

gis	-geon	-gel
register	surgeon	angel

-gic	-gy	gest
magic	energy	digestion
tragic		suggest

The words *angle* and *angel* are often confused. If you remember that *ge* has the soft sound, /j/, you will spell the words correctly.

Circle the soft-g sound. Write each word next to its definition.

angle	A heavenly being — *angel*
an(gel)	The space between two lines that meet — *angle*

Proofing Practice: Two common List 32 words are misspelled in each of the sentences below. Correct them as shown.

1. There was a ~~tragie~~ plane crash in the mountainous ~~rejen~~ of Colorado.   *tragic   region*
2. That energetic ~~jentulman~~ is a secret ~~ajent~~ for the FBI.   *gentleman   agent*
3. Islam is the major ~~relijon~~ of ~~Ejipt~~.   *religion   Egypt*
4. The ~~surjun jeneral~~ has determined that cigarette smoking is dangerous to your health.   *surgeon general*

WORKSHEET 32-M

Complete each sentence with the word from below that can be used in place of the italicized words. Use a dictionary to look up the meaning of unfamiliar words. Write the words in the puzzle.

submerged	longevity	ingenious	enraged	geology
pungent	generous	contingent	genie	legislates
fugitive				indulge

1. Our plans for a picnic tomorrow are *dependent* upon pleasant weather. (2 Down)
2. We often *yield to the wishes* of people who are sick. (10 Down)
3. The murderer was a *runaway* from justice. (6 Down)
4. The lion was *angered* by the kids who poked sticks at him. (5 Across)
5. Congress *makes laws* for the United States. (7 Down)
6. The *sharp* smell of the cheese made my nose wrinkle. (11 Across)
7. When Aladdin rubbed his lamp, the *magic spirit* appeared. (1 Down)
8. Good habits promote *long life*. (3 Across)
9. It was very *kind* of Gerald to donate his books to the school library. (4 Down)
10. Their *clever and inventive* escape plan was discovered. (8 Across)
11. My favorite course was *the study of the earth's crust*. (12 Across)
12. The house was *put under water* by the flood. (9 Across)

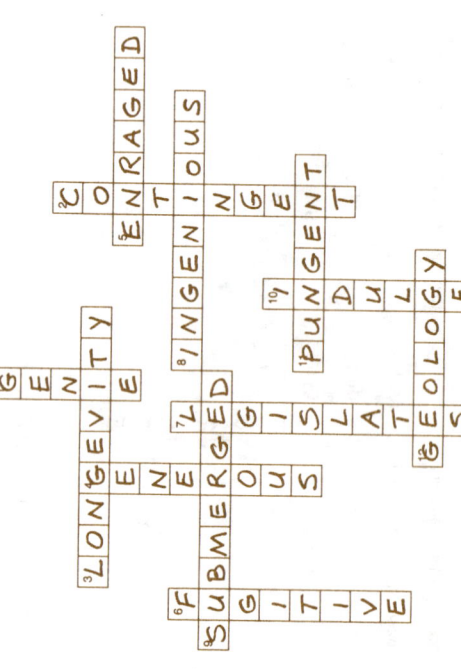

WORKSHEET 32-N

Fill in each blank with a word from below that makes sense in the sentence.

agent	gymnasium	original	energy	eligible
gestures	allergic	surgeon	dingy	vegetable
register				generate

1. The football players had to pass all subjects to be __eligible__ for the team.
2. Keep your thermostat at 65 degrees. You shouldn't waste __energy__.
3. Virginia bought this dress at a sale. It was marked down ten dollars from its __original__ price.
4. Babies who are __allergic__ to milk are fed a soy formula.
5. We need to __generate__ some new ideas for fundraising.
6. The speaker used a lot of __gestures__ when she talked.
7. The basement was dark and __dingy__.
8. Which __surgeon__ performed your operation?
9. Georgine must __register__ to vote before the election.
10. Beans, squash, and corn are sold at the __vegetable__ stand.
11. The basketball game will be held in the school __gymnasium__.
12. James Bond is a secret __agent__ in books and movies.

Unscramble the words below and spell them correctly in the blanks and circles. All the words can be found above.

GUNROSE   SUR(G)EO(N)
ILLGRACE   A(L)LERG(I)C
RIGTREES   RE(G)(I)STER

Unscramble the letters you have written in the circles to make another word from the list above:

ORIGINAL

VrV If an accented vowel-r combination is followed by a vowel, the first vowel has a modified long-vowel sound. Learn these sounds:

*ar*V says /air/ as in *care*.
*ir*V says /eer/ as in *spirit*.
*er*V says /eer/ as in *here* and /air/ as in *there*.
*ur*V says /yoor/ as in *cure*.

VrrV The VrV sound patterns also apply when the vowels *a, e,* and *i* are followed by two *r*'s and a vowel.

*arr*V says /air/ as in *carry*.
*err*V says /air/ as in *berry*.
*irr*V says /eer/ as in *mirror*.

In the following words, circle all the VrV and VrrV patterns. Then circle the sound(s) that they may have. Refer to the list above. Be careful—some of the vowel-*r* combinations may be followed by a consonant and have the *r*-controlled sound.

cereal	/eer/	/air/	/yoor/	variable	/eer/	/air/ /yoor/
security	/eer/	/air/	/yoor/	secretary	/eer/	/air/ /yoor/
merit	/eer/	/air/	/yoor/	purify	/eer/	/air/ /yoor/
department	/eer/	/air/	/yoor/	partner	/eer/	/air/ /yoor/
sterilize	/eer/	/air/	/yoor/	irregular	/eer/	/air/ /yoor/
spirit	/eer/	/air/	/yoor/	stereo	/eer/	/air/ /yoor/
charity	/eer/	/air/	/yoor/	sheriff	/eer/	/air/ /yoor/
clerical	/eer/	/air/	/yoor/	experiment	/eer/	/air/ /yoor/
murmur	/eer/	/air/	/yoor/	perturb	/eer/	/air/ /yoor/
period	/eer/	/air/	/yoor/	accuracy	/eer/	/air/ /yoor/
parakeet	/eer/	/air/	/yoor/	virile	/eer/	/air/ /yoor/
mercury	/eer/	/air/	/yoor/	series	/eer/	/air/ /yoor/
miracle	/eer/	/air/	/yoor/	surplus	/eer/	/air/ /yoor/
servant	/eer/	/air/	/yoor/	parallel	/eer/	/air/ /yoor/
irrigate	/eer/	/air/	/yoor/	permanent	/eer/	/air/ /yoor/

50

Read the following sentences and circle all the List 32 words that you can find.

1. The energetic German passenger lost his luggage in Georgetown.
2. Garrett and Ellie were going to Egypt to continue their studies in geology after college.
3. The clergyman's allergy caused him to have sinus congestion.
4. The agent suggested that he had been on an urgent and dangerous journey.
5. The messenger was genuinely sorry that he had brought tragic news.
6. The dangerous fugitive managed to avoid capture in rural Georgia.
7. General Page was eligible for a pension when he retired from his regiment.
8. The painting of the giraffe was an original genuine work of art.
9. The surgeon's handwriting was not at all legible.
10. Angela used her imagination when she read legends about giants, angels, and genies.
11. Genevieve's gymnastics team performed an energetic routine in the college gymnasium.

Look at List 32. Choose five words and write them in sentences below.

Sentences — Teacher corrected.

_____

_____

_____

_____

_____

Take out a piece of blank paper. Your teacher will dictate three of the sentences above for you to write.

You have completed the worksheets for List 32. Now it is time to check your accuracy in reading and spelling. Read and spell ten words selected by your teacher, and record your scores on the Accuracy Checklist. Work toward 90–100 percent accuracy.

When you have achieved 90–100 percent accuracy in reading, build up your reading speed. Decide on your rate goal with your teacher. Record your rate on the Proficiency Graph.

My goal for reading List 32 is _____ words per minute with two or fewer errors.

48

WORKSHEET 33–B

Your teacher will dictate syllables from words that contain the sounds /eer/, /air/, and /yoor/. Say the syllables aloud as you spell them, using the guides. The final vowel symbol (V) is written in for you.

Part 1

Use *arV* to spell /air/.
Use *irV* to spell /eer/.
Use *urV* to spell /yoor/.

1. par V
2. mir V
3. cur V
4. spir V
5. var V
6. bar V
7. pur V
8. vir V
9. char V
10. bur V
11. har V
12. fur V

Part 2

Use *erV* to spell /eer/.

1. her V
2. ser V
3. ter V
4. per V
5. mer V
6. fer V

Part 3

Use *erV* to spell /air/.

1. ther V
2. der V
3. mer V
4. per V
5. her V
6. ster V
7. cler V
8. ver V

Review: /air/ can be spelled __arV__ or __erV__ in VrV words.
/eer/ can be spelled __irV__ or __erV__ in VrV words.

WORKSHEET 33–C

Pronounce and combine the syllables. Then cover the divided word and practice reading the whole word. Underline the VrV pattern in the whole word.

arV = /air/

ap par ent	apparent
par a keet	parakeet
par al lel	parallel
par a graph	paragraph
par a chute	parachute
com par i son	comparison
dis par i ty	disparity
char ac ter	character
bar o met ric	barometric

erV = /air/

ker o sene	kerosene
ther a py	therapy
cler i cal	clerical
ster il ize	sterilize
ster e o	stereo
in her it	inherit
pros per i ty	prosperity
ger i at ric	geriatric
im per a tive	imperative
hys ter i cal	hysterical
cer e mo ny	ceremony
der i va tion	derivation

erV = /eer/

ser ies	series
cer e al	cereal
mere ly	merely
ex per i ence	experience
man a ger i al	managerial
in ter fer ence	interference

irV = /eer/

vir ile	virile
spir i tu al	spiritual
mir a cle	miracle
ir as ci ble	irascible
mir ac u lous	miraculous
con spir a cy	conspiracy

urV = /yoor/

se cure	secure
fig ure	figure
pur i ty	purity
mer cu ry	mercury
ac cur a cy	accuracy
se cur i ty	security
bu reau	bureau

WORKSHEET 33–D

Match the syllables to make real words. Say each word aloud as you write it.

fur ro	hero	par iff	sheriff
he it	spirit	ur ror	mirror
ter y	fury	mir ine	urine
spir ror	terror	sher ent	parent

cher row	arrow	ze rot	carrot
her ry	cherry	mere ro	zero
sin ring	herring	spar row	sparrow
ar cere	sincere	car ly	merely

Unscramble these multisyllabic words.

per ex ence i	experience
ment i per ex	experiment
y re sec tar	secretary
di or y nar	ordinary
o tion ar lu rev y	revolutionary
ize il ster	sterilize

Find and circle the twenty-two words above in the puzzle below. The words can be found in a straight line across or up and down.

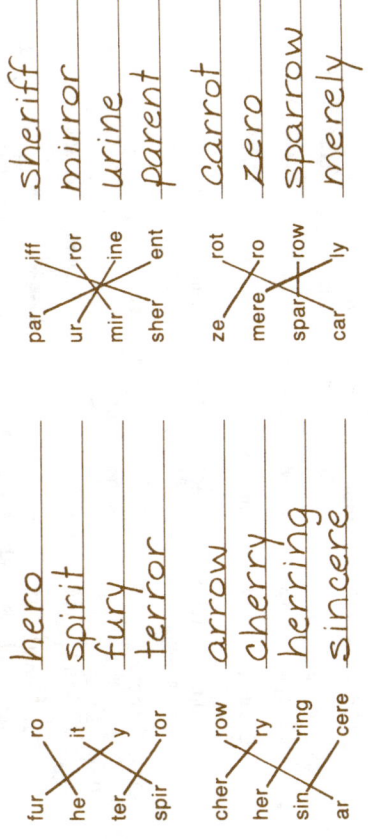

53

WORKSHEET 33–E

Your teacher will dictate some words. Sound out each word as you write the missing syllable(s). Then write the words under the correct heading. To help with syllabication and spelling, the final vowel and the doubled r of the combination are already written in for you.

/air/ is spelled *ar*V or *arr*V.
/eer/ is spelled *ir*V or *irr*V.
/yoor/ is spelled *ur*V.

*1. __par__ ent
*2. __mir__ ror
*3. __car__ rot
*4. se __cur__ i ty
*5. __char__ i ty
*6. __mir__ a cle

*7. __nar__ row
8. __ir__ reg u __lar__
*9. ac __cur__ a cy
*10. __par__ a __graph__
*11. char __ac__ ter
12. __ir__ re __sist__ i ble

*ar*V and *arr*V words
Parent
Carrot
charity
narrow
Paragraph
character

*ir*V and *irr*V words
mirror
miracle
irregular
irresistible

*ur*V words
security
accuracy

Have another student test you on spelling the starred words. They are practical spelling words.

My score: _____ words correct.

54

/eer/ at the end of multisyllabic words is usually spelled *ere*. Fill in the blanks with *ere* and write the whole word. Then write the words in alphabetical order.

	Copy	ABC Order
*h _ere_	here	here
*se v_ere_	severe	interfere
re v_ere_	revere	merely
*m_ere_ ly	merely	persevere
*sin c_ere_ ly	sincerely	revere
*in ter t_ere_	interfere	severe
per se v_ere_	persevere	sincerely

per says /peer/

pros _per_ ity
per iscope → periscope
per iodical → periodical

per followed by a vowel can say /pair/ or /peer/. Fill in the blanks with *per* and copy the words under the correct heading below.

per says /pair/	*per* says /peer/
peril	experience
prosperity	period
periscope	periodical

*ex _per_ ience
*ex _per_ iment
im _per_ ative

*ex _per_ ilous
*ex _per_ iod
per ish
per il

experiment
imperative
perilous
perish

peril
prosperity
periscope

Have another student test you on spelling the starred words. They are practical spelling words.

My score: _____ words correct.

56

The following patterns for the /air/ sound are spelled *erV*.

terr followed by a vowel is pronounced /tair/. Fill in the blanks with *terr*. Then write each word next to its definition.

terr itory	1. Question thoroughly	interrogate
terr ible	2. A raised level of land	terrace
terr or	3. Awful	terrible
terr ier	4. Fear	terror
terr ace	5. To scare	terrify
in terr ogate	6. A kind of dog	terrier
terr ify	7. Land; region	territory

her or *herr* followed by a vowel is pronounced /hair/. Fill in the blanks with *her*. Then write each word next to its definition.

her etic	8. A wading bird with a long neck	heron
her oin	9. A very brave girl or woman	heroine
her ring	10. An addictive drug	heroin
in her it	11. Birthright; something handed down from the past	heritage
her on	12. A person who holds a belief different from the accepted belief	heretic
her oine	13. To receive as an heir	inherit
her itage	14. Type of fish	herring

ster followed by a vowel is pronounced /stair/. Fill in the blanks with *ster*. Then write each word next to its definition.

ster eo	15. To free from germs; to make barren, not fertile	sterilize
ster ilize	16. Out of control; unnaturally excited	hysterical
hy ster ical	17. A non-individualized statement about a group	stereotype
ster eotype	18. Sound system	stereo

55

Words that contain the VrV combination divide after the r and follow other syllabication rules.
Divide these words into syllables and note the accent patterns.*

The primary accent is on the syllable just before the ending -ic.

geriatric   ger i [at] ric

barometric   bar o met ric

characteristic   char ac ter [is] tic

The primary accent is on the syllable just before the ending -tion.

derivation   der i [va] tion

irritation   ir ri [ta] tion

sterilization   ster il i [za] tion

verification   ver i fi [ca] tion

The primary accent is on the syllable just before the ending -ity.

purity   [pur] i ty

charity   [char] i ty

security   se [cur] i ty

sincerity   sin [cer] i ty

irresponsibility   ir re spon si [bil] i ty

*A Summary of Accent Patterns is on pages 69 and 70.

---

erV has two sounds, /air/ and /eer/. Divide these erV words into syllables. Then copy them by syllables under the correct heading below.

period	merit	clerical	errand	verify
zero	interference	cafeteria	prosperity	series
kerosene	error	experience	cereal	experiment

erV says /air/

mer	it		
er	rand		
er	ror		
cler	i	cal	
ver	i	fy	
ker	o	sene	
pros	per	i	ty
ex	per	i	ment

erV says /eer/

ze	ro			
ser	ies			
per	i	od		
cer	e	al		
in	ter	fer	ence	
ex	per	i	ence	
caf	e	ter	i	a

Review: The two sounds of erV are /air/ and /eer/.

Unscramble the words below and spell them correctly in the blanks and circles. All the words can be found above.

RICECALL   CL(E)RICA(L)

TIMER   M(E)R(I)T

SIRSEE   SE(R)IES

IRACEFATE   (C)AFETERI(A)

Unscramble the letters you have written in the circles to make another word from above.

CEREAL

The combination -ary is found at the end of words and says /air ē/. Fill in the blanks with ary and write the words by syllables as you read them. Notice the accent patterns.* Then practice reading the words below to build up your speed.

prim **ary**	▢ Pri	mar	y
Febru **ary**	▢ Feb	ru	ar'	y
diction **ary**	▢ dic	tio	nar'	y
secret **ary**	▢ sec	re	tar'	y
tempor **ary**	▢ tem	po	rar'	y
mercen **ary**	▢ mer	ce	nar'	y
coron **ary**	▢ cor	o	nar'	y
milit **ary**	▢ mil	i	tar'	y
tribut **ary**	▢ trib	u	tar'	y
ordin **ary**	▢ or	di	nar'	y
second **ary**	▢ sec	on	dar'	y
sanit **ary**	▢ san	i	tar'	y
vocabul **ary**	vo	▢ cab	u	lar'	y
revolution **ary**	▢ rev	o	▢ lu	tio	nar'	y

▢ = syllable with primary accent
___ = syllable with secondary accent

59

The pattern arr is found in some common words. Complete the words below by adding arr. Then fill in each blank with the correct word.

c **arr** y	1. A talking bird	parrot
*c **arr** ot	2. A small, singing bird	sparrow
*p **arr** ot	3. Overly proud, "stuck-up"	arrogant
* **arr** ow	4. An orange vegetable	carrot
*n **arr** ow	5. →; a bow and ___	arrow
*sp **arr** ow	6. Opposite of wide	narrow
arr ogant	7. To wed; to join as husband and wife	marry
L **arr** y	8. A vehicle with wheels	carriage
*m **arr** y	9. A boy's name	Larry
c **arr** iage	10. Act of marrying	marriage
*m **arr** iage	11. To take from one place to another	carry

The patterns bar and barr are often found in words. Complete the words by adding bar and barr. Then fill in each blank with the correct word.

bar **r** acks	12. Relating to air pressure	barometric
bar **r** itone	13. To obstruct with a barrier	barricade
ba **r** ometric	14. A male voice	baritone
bar **r** icade	15. A wooden container	barrel
bar **r** acuda	16. A fierce fish	barracuda
bar **r** ier	17. Something that stands in the way	barrier
*bar **r** el	18. A building that soldiers live in	barracks

Have another student test you on spelling the starred words. They are practical spelling words.

My score: _____ words correct

60

/eer/ at the beginning of a word is usually spelled *irr*. Often *irr* is a variation of the prefix *in-*, meaning "not." Change the phrases below into *irr* words.

1. not regular → *irregular*
2. not rational → *irrational*
3. not responsible → *irresponsible*
4. not resistible → *irresistible*
5. not reducible → *irreducible*
6. not refutable → *irrefutable*
7. not relevant → *irrelevant*
8. not reversible → *irreversible*
9. not replaceable → *irreplaceable*
10. not retrievable → *irretrievable*

Add *irr* to the word parts below, copy the words, and write them in alphabetical order.

	Copy	ABC Order
irr igate	*irrigate*	*irrigable*
irr itable	*irritable*	*irrigate*
irr itate	*irritate*	*irrigation*
irr igation	*irrigation*	*irritable*
irr itation	*irritation*	*irritant*
irr igable	*irrigable*	*irritate*
irr itant	*irritant*	*irritation*

Four of the words above are in the same family and have to do with "annoying." Write them.

irritable   irritate   irritation   irritant

Three of the words have to do with "watering the land." The words are:

irrigate   irrigation   irrigable

In the following words, change *y* to *i* and add the suffix.

marry + age = *marriage*
carry + age = *carriage*
vary + able = *variable*
vary + ous = *various*

When a root ends in silent *e*, drop the *e* before adding a vowel suffix.

Add suffixes to the following roots. You may have to add, drop, or change some letters. Check a dictionary if you are not sure.

pure + ly = *purely*
pure + ify = *purify*
spirit + al = *spiritual*
irrigate + tion = *irrigation*
prosper + ity = *prosperity*
secure + ly = *securely*
secure + ity = *security*
miracle + ous = *miraculous*
conspire + acy = *conspiracy*
hero + ic = *heroic*

Find and circle the fourteen words above in the puzzle below. Check to see that you spelled them correctly. They can be found in a straight line across or up and down.

```
P R O S P E R I T Y P H S P I R I T U A L N
U M I R A C U L O U S E C U R I T Y E F D B
R O M A R R I A G E Q R T R R I G A T I O N
E V A R I A B L E C F O T I V A R I O U S L
L M S E C U R E L Y K I S F R E A I J H G C
Y Z W C O N S P I R A C Y C A R R I A G E
```

WORKSHEET 33–N

Your teacher will dictate practical spelling words that contain *VrV* combinations. Repeat each word aloud, decide which list it belongs in, and spell the word, sounding each syllable aloud.

/air/ (spelled *ar*V)
charity
character

/air/ (spelled *er*V)
stereo
America

/air/ (spelled *arr*V)
merry
terrible

/eer/ (spelled *ir*V)
miracle

/eer/ (spelled *err*V)
cereal
period
cafeteria
sincere
experience

/eer/ (spelled *irr*V)
irritate

/yoor/ (spelled *ur*V)
secure

Proofing Practice: Two common List 33 words are misspelled in each of the sentences below. Correct them as shown.

1. The ~~sheriff~~ had a terrible scare when the ~~kerosene~~ leaked in the cafeteria.   sheriff   kerosene
2. In ~~January~~ the weather near Lake Erie is often very ~~severe~~.   January   severe
3. Sarah's ~~parents~~ think that parakeets make better pets than ~~parrots~~ or sparrows.   Parents   parrots
4. Harold was tired of ~~clerical~~ work and wanted to become a ~~security~~ guard.   clerical   security
5. Karen made many ~~errors~~ because she rarely looked up new ~~vocabulary~~ words in a   errors   vocabulary
dictionary.

63

WORKSHEET 33–O

Write the correct word from below next to its definition. Use a dictionary to look up the meanings of unfamiliar words.

virile	parasite	revere	perilous	coronary
conspiracy	imperative	arrogant	irascible	geriatrics
interrogate	erudite	verify	prosperity	barbarian

1. Overly proud; haughty — arrogant
2. Success; having enough money — prosperity
3. A plot; secret planning — conspiracy
4. To love and respect deeply — revere
5. Full of manly strength and masculine vigor — virile
6. To prove something to be true — verify
7. Dangerous — perilous
8. Having to do with the heart — coronary
9. To question somebody formally — interrogate
10. An uncivilized person — barbarian
11. Urgent; necessary — imperative
12. Scholarly; learned — erudite
13. An animal or plant that lives on another from which it gets its food — parasite
14. Easily made angry; irritable — irascible
15. The study of old age and its diseases — geriatrics

64

Complete the puzzle, using the words below. Use a dictionary to look up the meanings of unfamiliar words.

vary	dictionary	mercenary	military	sanitary
primary	secretary	coronary	tributary	vocabulary
February	temporary		ordinary	revolutionary

Across

1. Relating to a complete, radical change
3. A reference book
8. A stream or river that runs into a larger body of water
9. A person who types, takes dictation, and keeps records
11. A list of words and definitions
12. For a short time
13. First in order
14. Soldiers; army

Down

2. The usual
4. Relating to the heart
5. The second month of the year
6. Relating to doing things only for the money
7. Not dirty
10. To change

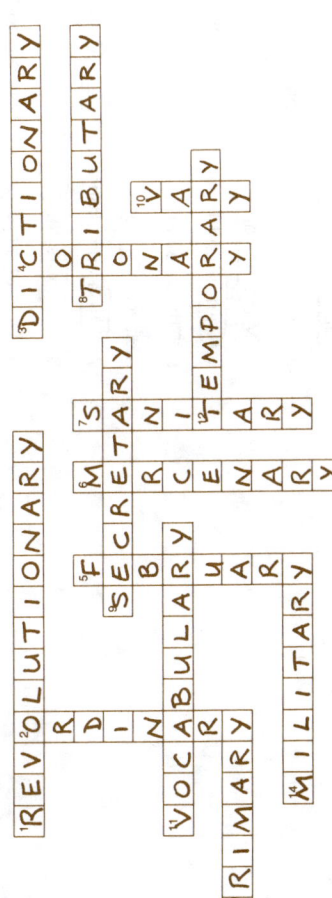

65

Fill in each blank with a word from below that makes sense in the sentence.

vary	sanitary	ceremony	perilous	persevere
cereal	sterilize	arrogant	irrigate	barometric
terrace				interrogate

1. Most people try to avoid Eric because he is so _arrogant_. It's no fun being with someone who thinks he is the greatest.
2. The lawyer had to _interrogate_ the suspect to prepare for the trial.
3. When some people get frustrated, they tend to give up rather than to _persevere_.
4. Sherry likes to eat _cereal_ and milk for breakfast.
5. Climbing Mt. Everest is _perilous_, but many people have succeeded in conquering its heights.
6. In order for crops to grow in the desert, it is necessary to _irrigate_.
7. Sarah and Harold had their wedding _ceremony_ on the park _terrace_.
8. The weather in March can _vary_ greatly. Sometimes it snows, and other times it is really warm.
9. The _barometric_ pressure just dropped. It will probably rain tomorrow.
10. The utensils are not _sanitary_. You will have to _sterilize_ them to kill the germs.

Find and circle the twelve words above in the puzzle below. The words can be found in a straight line across or up and down.

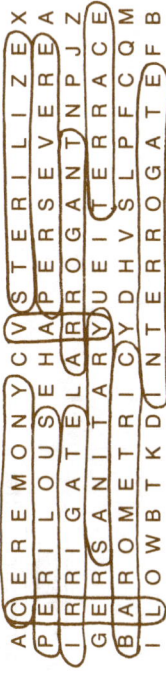

66

WORKSHEET 33–R

Read the following sentences and circle all the List 33 words that you can find.

1. (Barry) and (Carol) went to (Paris) to get (married.)

2. It would be quite (irresponsible) of (Mary) to poke a hole in that (parachute.)

3. Ms (Carrington's) gifts to (charity) were one example of her (generous) (character)

4. (Garrett) and Ellie were (wary) of the (barracudas.)

5. They are selling (carrot) cake and (cherry) pie in the (cafeteria) today.

6. It really (irritates) me when (Terrance) plays his (stereo) so loudly.

7. (Terrie) complained to (Sheriff) (Clarence) about the (terrible) (security) in the jail.

8. We (figure) that (Karen) will hire a new (secretary) in (February.)

9. Only a (miracle) could have saved (Carrie) from that (terrible) (experience.)

10. (Marion) became (hysterical) when (Sharon) spilled (kerosene) on the (terrace)

11. (Perry) was quite (sincere) about his (revolutionary) ideas.

Look at List 33. Choose five words and write them in sentences below.

Sentences – Teacher corrected.

_____

_____

_____

_____

Take out a piece of blank paper. Your teacher will dictate three of the sentences above for you to write.

You have completed the worksheets for List 33. Now it is time to check your accuracy in reading and spelling. Read and spell ten words selected by your teacher, and record your scores on the Accuracy Checklist. Work toward 90–100 percent accuracy.

When you have achieved 90–100 percent accuracy in reading, build up your reading speed. Decide on your rate goal with your teacher. Record your rate on the Proficiency Graph.

My goal for reading List 33 is _____ words per minute with two or fewer errors.

ACCURACY CHECKLIST

Megawords 6, Lists 30–33

Student _____

Record accuracy score as a fraction: $\dfrac{\text{\# correct}}{\text{\# attempted}}$

List	Examples	Check Test Scores Date:		Reading			Spelling		
		Reading	Spelling						
30. Sounds of *ch*, *ph*, and *que*	chronicle orphanage								
31. Soft *c*	necessary anticipate								
32. Soft *g*	vegetable tragedy								
33. Vowel-*r*-Vowel Combinations	experience parallel								
Review: Lists 30–33									

PROFICIENCY GRAPH

Student_____

Goal_____

●━━━━━● Words Read Correctly

✕━━━━✕ Errors

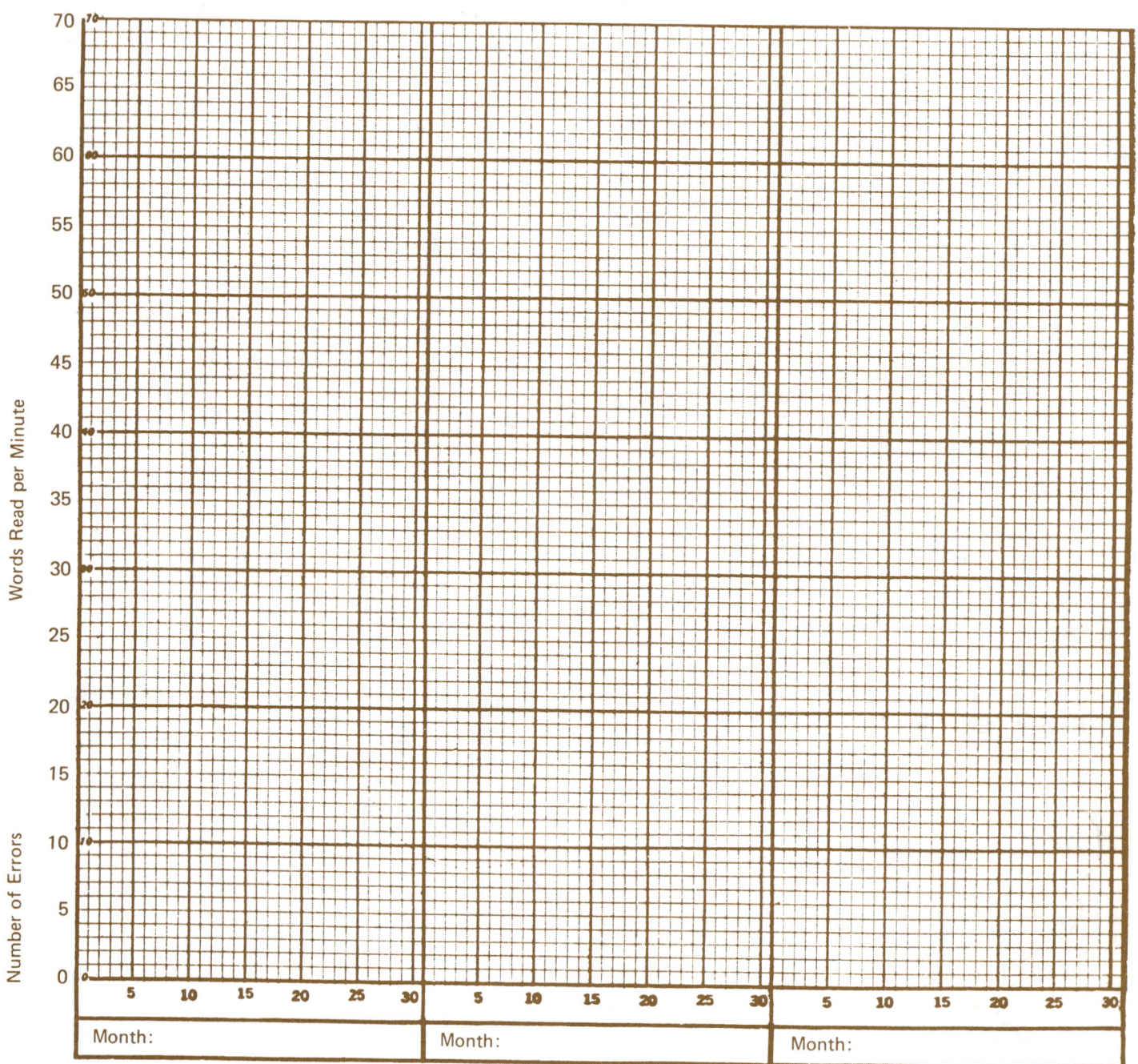

Calendar Days

30. schedule

technique

chivalry

atmosphere

technical

31. accelerator

icicle

facilitate

decisive

participate

32. exaggerate

legislation

gigantic

energetic

gymnastics

33. sterilize

experiment

disparity

conspiracy

accuracy